Warman's
Dolls
FIELD GUIDE

Dawn Herlocher

Values and Identification

©2006 by Krause Publications

Published by

krause publications

An Imprint of F+W Publications

700 East State Street • Iola, WI 54990-0001
715-445-2214 • 888-457-2873

Our toll-free number to place an order or obtain
a free catalog is (800) 258-0929.

Library of Congress Catalog Number: 2005935189
ISBN 10-digit: 0-87349-983-2
ISBN 13-digit: 978-0-87349-983-5

Designed by Marilyn McGrane
Edited by Mary Sieber

Printed in China

Contents

Introduction

There is probably no rational explanation for the feelings collectors have for their dolls. Perhaps it's because they awaken memories and dreams, stirring our feelings of nostalgia, or the simple pleasure gained in admiring the beauty of these present-day reminders of a long vanished era.

The attraction to dolls seems to be immediate and universal, made obvious by the thousands of new enthusiasts who have excitedly embraced the world of doll collecting in recent years.

No two dolls are exactly alike. A study of their various features indicates the factors that influence the value of a doll, including rarity, condition, quality of material, artistry, availability, originality, history of providence, and the ever-important visual appeal. All of these factors contribute to a doll's charisma.

Please take the time to thoroughly inspect a doll. An antique bisque doll head should be checked not only on the outside, but also from the inside, for at times a repair or hairline crack will only be visible from the inside. Remember not to confuse maintenance with repairs. Reset eyes, restrung bodies, and patched leather are examples of necessary maintenance and are not repairs to a doll. Modern dolls should always be in perfect, complete condition. Inspect the markings of a doll. You may find them on the back of the head, the torso, the bottom of a foot, or even on the derriere. Of course, many fine dolls will have absolutely no markings. Learn from every doll you see or handle, for there is almost as much fun in learning about a doll as there is in owning it. Visit doll shows and museums.

I encourage you to read and study as much as you can about dolls. The two volumes of Dorothy S., Elizabeth A., and Evelyn J.

29" Kestner #146, $1,850; **28" Heinrich Handwerck** with slit fur brows, $1,600; and **24" Kley & Hahn Walküre**, $1,100. Courtesy of David Cobb Auction

Coleman's *The Collector's Encyclopedia of Dolls* (Crown Publishing 1972 and 1986) are accurate guidebooks to doll manufacturing prior to 1930. *Antique Trader's Doll Makers and Marks* (Krause Publications, 1999) is a concise directory for doll identification. If you don't own a copy, visit a library that does.

Talk to other collectors. I have never met a doll collector who doesn't enjoy talking about his or her dolls. Consider joining a doll club. Clubs that are members of the United Federation of Doll Clubs (U.F.D.C.) "represent the highest standards of excellence for collectors to create, stimulate and maintain interest in all matters pertaining to doll collecting." Write the U.F.D.C. at P.O. Box 14146, Parkville, MO 64152 to obtain the address of a club near you.

Collecting Tips

The following procedures are provided to inform and educate. Neither the author nor publisher accept liability nor responsibility in respect to any type of loss or damage caused, or alleged to be caused, directly or indirectly, by the information or products contained in this book. We simply intend to share some old tricks and methods that have been used over the years.

Dolls require tender loving care. They need to be repaired, restored, handled, displayed, and stored properly. The following tips will help you develop skills to ensure that your dolls receive the loving treatment they deserve.

When restoring a doll, the best approach is to be a minimalist. Do only the bare minimum to bring a doll to display level—retain, rather than destroy. Period features count heavily in a doll's value. Plan any repairs in a step-by-step process, evaluating as you go along.

Always approach the cleaning or maintenance of dolls with the greatest of care and respect. If you're not sure how to perform a certain procedure, ask an expert. We have an obligation to future doll collectors to preserve the dolls in our care and to maintain them in as good or better condition than they were when we received them.

Doll Care

Bisque, China, Porcelain

Bisque, china, and parian are all made of clay, feldspar, and flint. Differences between them are subtle. Parian is unglazed, untinted porcelain; china is glazed porcelain; and bisque is unglazed porcelain with a flesh color.

The earliest bisque, china, and parian dolls were pressed into a mold by hand; later examples were poured.

Cleaning porcelain is fairly simple. The decorations have been fired on, so it is highly unlikely that you will harm them by cleaning. Start with the least-abrasive technique—usually warm soapy water. If this is not sufficient, try a wet eraser. As a last resort, very gently clean with a low-abrasive cleaner such as Tilex® or Soft Scrub®. Use extreme caution, as some cleansers contain bleaching agents that are devastating to antique clothing, wigs, or bodies. When displaying a bisque, china, or parian doll, avoid the damaging ultraviolet rays of direct sunlight.

If placed on a doll stand, be sure that the doll is secure and that the stand is weighted sufficiently to support it.

Celluloid

Celluloid dolls are extremely perishable. They are easily broken and become quite brittle over time. Proper care and respect of a celluloid doll helps a perfect example remain in that condition. Heat is celluloid's worst enemy. Keep these dolls in a cool room with good ventilation, and never store celluloid in a sealed case—it is highly combustible.

24" Belton-type #137, $5,200, and **20" Gebruder Kuhnlenz #30,** $6,800. Courtesy of David Cobb Auction

Cloth

Cloth dolls have a special place in every doll collector's heart. Even a well-loved rag doll tugs at one's heartstrings. Vintage and even the not-so-vintage cloth art dolls can be valued at thousands of dollars. They deserve your best efforts to preserve them and prevent needless deterioration.

Clean fabric is a prerequisite to preservation. Exposing a doll to any pollutants through storage or display weakens the fabric. Direct sunlight is an enemy of cloth dolls and should be avoided.

Inspect cloth dolls regularly for signs of insect activity. Insecticides designed especially for textiles are available under several brand names. When used according to the manufacturer's instructions, the results can be excellent.

If you decide to vacuum your doll, place a nylon screen over the fabric first to protect delicate fibers. Often, a thorough vacuuming is enough to restore a doll to display condition. Again, approach this procedure with appropriate caution. If a valuable or historically significant cloth doll is badly soiled, seek the advice of a professional who specializes in textile conservation.

Some stains on cloth dolls can be removed with an eraser—art gum or tapeten appear to give the best results. Use this technique with careful, gentle application. Frequently stains, such as ink, may be removed with hair spray. It is essential to test the fabric first on an inconspicuous location to assure that no damage will occur. Apply the hair spray with a cloth, then wipe in a light rubbing motion using a clean white cloth.

Lenci once advertised that a Lenci doll could be cleaned by rubbing it with a piece of bread!

To preserve and display cloth dolls, it is best to keep them in protective cases and inspect them regularly. Moth crystals should be placed near your dolls. Many collectors recommend making a small cloth pouch, filling it with moth crystals, cedar chips, or whole cloves, and placing it under the doll's hat or tying it around its waist beneath the clothing.

Composition & Papier-Mâché

Composition and papier-mâché dolls, being made from pulp-based materials, require similar care. They are particularly susceptible to damage from temperature and humidity changes. Never store composition or papier-mâché dolls in a hot or cold attic or in a damp basement.

Most collectors will accept slight signs of aging on composition dolls—fine craze lines or crackled eyes, for example. Think long and hard before performing irreversible restorations that can compromise a doll's historical and practical value. Remember a well-done restoration is one that can later be undone. Temporary cover-ups are best.

There are several popular methods for cleaning composition. Test any method first on an inconspicuous area of the doll. Work quickly. Never leave any substance on the surface for any length of time. Pond's® Cold Cream or Vaseline® and a soft tissue are favorites of many collectors. Another option is paste window cleaner—not the ammonia type, but the old fashioned paste available at most hardware stores.

Wigs can be restyled after lightly spraying with Johnson's® baby shampoo detangling formula, carefully working out the tangles. Faded or worn-off facial features can be touched up with artist's colored pencils; when moistened they are quite easy to apply. Crackled eyes are best left alone.

Plastic, Rubber, Metal & Other Synthetic Materials

Hard plastic dolls are a favorite with collectors. Their sharp features and beautiful detailing are hard to resist.

Hard plastic is very resilient and can be cleaned with warm soapy water. Stubborn stains may be removed with cold cream or waterless hand cleaner. Avoid chlorine bleach and ammonia. Facial features may not be as durable, so approach painted surfaces with caution, checking paint stability before proceeding. Never use fingernail polish remover or lacquer thinner, which may eat into the plastic.

Many report excellent results using Oxy-10 to remove stains that are not close to painted surfaces. Moisten a cotton ball and allow it to sit on the stain for a few minutes. You may need to repeat this process several times. After each cleaning, wash the doll with mild soap and rinse well.

When displaying or storing hard plastic dolls, avoid direct exposure to ultraviolet light. Though seemingly indestructible, hard plastic can slowly oxidize and change color. Direct heat may also cause warping.

Rubber, early latex, or Magic Skin dolls will deteriorate no matter what precautions are taken, but you may be able to delay the process. Any form of grease is harmful and accelerates deterioration. Always wear cotton gloves when handling a Magic Skin doll. I practice the old trick of rubbing corn starch on these dolls twice a year—once on my March birthday and once on my father's September birthday. As with all dolls, maintain an even temperature and relative humidity.

Tin dolls often have chipped paint. When the metal becomes very cold, the paint lifts easily from the surface. Store or display metal dolls in an environment with a relatively constant temperature.

Vinyl dolls are probably the most lifelike in appearance and touch. Special care is needed to keep them looking good. Extreme room temperatures are harmful. Even quality vinyl dolls subjected to heaters or air conditioners can be damaged in just a few months. Direct sunlight can be devastating. Vinyl is also sensitive to fluorescent lighting; use indirect non-fluorescent lights. Finally, avoid tightly sealed showcases or glass domes, as condensation can form and damage vinyl dolls.

Wood

Wooden dolls have withstood the test of time quite well, as proven by the sheer number that have survived the years. Chipping paint is a major problem with wooden dolls. Humidity and mistreatment are the two main culprits. Keep wooden dolls in a dry atmosphere. Expanding and contracting associated with high humidity causes paint to chip. Knocks and bumps can also chip paint, so take care in moving or displaying wooden dolls.

Wax

Wax dolls tend to intimidate many collectors. They do require special care, as do all types of dolls. Basic care and common sense will help preserve a wax doll in perfect condition. Of course, never place a wax doll in direct sunlight or near any heat source, such as a fireplace mantle.

A long-accepted practice for cleaning wax dolls is to start with the safest method and then gradually progress to more drastic measures until a suitable remedy is found. First, try a solution of cool water and Woolite®. Saturate a cotton ball or cotton swab and wash the wax. If this is unsuccessful, try a dab of cold cream on a cotton swab, followed by a rinse of the Woolite solution and then clean, cool water. As a last resort, try denatured alcohol on a cotton ball, followed by a thorough rinsing. Never use turpentine to clean wax dolls, as it can soften the wax.

Old Time Tips for Repairs and Preservation

Some longtime doll collectors have been known to place a drop of sewing machine oil in the crackled eyes of a composition doll. Although it does seem to make the eyes appear clearer for a time, the downside is that the oil dries and causes further deterioration. It is always evident when eyes have been treated in this manner.

Green deposits found around pierced ears in Barbie dolls are often corrected by covering the ears with a small piece of cotton soaked in Tarn-X® silver cleaner. Wrap the head in plastic wrap to keep the application moist. Check after two days—if the ears remain green, replace the plastic wrap. If the ears are still green after four days, repeat the procedure with fresh cotton balls. Once the green is gone, rub a paste of baking soda and water over the treated areas. After several days, flake off the dried baking soda and clean the area with warm, soapy water on a cotton swab. Tarn-X causes a chemical reaction that acts as a bleach; the baking soda neutralizes the reaction, and the warm, soapy water removes any residue. It is important to perform each step as described, and to inspect the doll periodically throughout the process.

Bubble Cut Barbies often have sticky or greasy faces. This is due to an ingredient emitted by the vinyl. To alleviate the problem, carefully remove the head from the body and clean inside and out with a cotton swab soaked in alcohol. Dry thoroughly, fill the head cavity with baking soda, and replace it on the body. The baking soda will neutralize the chemicals and absorb the extracted grease.

Here are a few fun old-fashioned tips suggested by doll collectors. They are neither recommended nor condemned. I have included them for your enjoyment only.

- To remove mildew: Soak in sour milk and salt, then lay the article in the sun. To remove the milk therapy, follow with a warm soapy water wash and rinse.
- To restore color to faded cloth: Sponge with chloroform.
- To soften and clean old kid leather: Saturate an old woolen rag with kerosene and rub into the kid.
- To clean old ivory: Scrub with Ivory soap; bleach in the sun for several days, reapplying the soapy solution often.
- To remove tar: Clean first with turpentine, then clean with Lux soap.
- To remove paint: Rub patiently with chloroform.
- To restore faded calico: Wash in water with a teaspoon of sugar of lead; soak for fifteen minutes and launder.
- Black taffeta is best washed in strong tea.

Dolls are a fascinating part of our culture and provide a look into our past. By scattering the seeds of doll collecting and furnishing basic information, I hope I've helped the reader to build a collection that is enjoyable and profitable.

Doll Clubs

Doll clubs are wonderful. Most are well organized and in constant pursuit of information. They are often involved in community services, making worthwhile contributions. Many clubs have conventions, luncheons, sales, newsletters, swap meets, and other activities all centered around dolls. The following list will help you find a doll club in your area.

Annalee Doll Society
P.O. Box 1137
Meredith, NH 03253-1137

**Antique Toy Collectors
of America**
Rt. 2, Box 5A
Parkton, MD 21120

**Cabbage Patch Kids
Collectors Club**
P.O. Box 714
Cleveland, GA 30528

Chatty Cathy Collectors Club
2610 Dover St.
Piscataway, NJ 08854-4437

Collectors' Information Bureau
77 W. Washington St.
Suite 1716
Chicago, IL 60602

Doll Artisan Guild
35 Main St.
Oneonta, NY 13820

Doll Collectors of America
14 Chestnut Rd.
Westford, MD 01886

Effanbee Dolls
4701 Queensbury Rd.
Riverdale, MD 20840

GI Joe Collectors Club
150 S. Glenoaks Blvd.
Burbank, CA 91510

Ginny Doll Club
9628 Hidden Oaks Circle
Tampa, FL 33612

Ideal Doll Collector's Club
P.O. Box 623
Lexington, MA 02173

International Barbie® Doll Club
P.O. Box 70
Bronx, NY 10464

International Doll Makers' Association
3364 Pine Creek Dr.
San Jose, CA 95132

International Rose O'Neill Club
P.O. Box 668
Branson, MO 65616

Madame Alexander Fan Club
P.O. Box 330
Mundelein, IL 60060

National Institute of American Doll Artists
303 Riley St.
Falls Church, VA 22046

National Organization of Miniaturists and Dollers
1300 Schroder
Normal, IL 61761

United Federation of Doll Clubs (UFDC)
P. O. Box 14146
Parkville MO 64152

Price Adjustment Factors

The most frequently asked question is how I determine the prices. It is really quite simple; I keep in constant contact with many doll dealers, auctioneers, show promoters, and brokers. The influences within the doll world have changed drastically over the years. We are indeed an international-global community. Dealers think nothing of flying to England for an opportunity to purchase dolls for an increasingly discriminating collecting pool. It is necessary, therefore, to consider the values assigned to dolls not only in this country, but also in England, Spain, Switzerland, Australia, and even France.

Prices in this book are based on dolls in good condition, appropriately dressed with no damage. Unfortunately, dolls frequently have a number of faults.

What follows is a method by which you can take the prices listed in this book and adjust them to fit the doll you are examining. Admittedly, some of these adjustments do require you to make a judgment call. When analyzing a doll, it's always best to use your head, not your heart. That may sound easy, but it is difficult to do. Over-grading a doll and, hence, overpaying for it, are major problems in doll collecting circles. Hopefully, the suggestions offered here will make you a wiser, more savvy buyer and/or seller.

Bisque

Hairline crack or repair in back or under wig .... **−50%**
Hairline crack or repair to face .... **−70%**
Very poor body (beyond normal wear) .... **−35%**
Replaced body.. **−45%**
Tinted or untinted ornamentation damage...................................... **−25%**
Original super-pristine condition and/or with original box ..**+200% or more**

China

Head cracked or repaired .... **−75%**
Cracked or repaired shoulder.. **−50%**
Worn or replaced body.. **−40%**
Exceptional, original doll .... **+75% or more**

Cloth

Face stained or faded .... **−50%**
Tears or large holes in face.. **−80%**
Mint or excellent condition ....**+200%**

Metal

Lightly dented or lightly chipped head .... **−50%**
Badly dented or badly chipped head .... **−80%**
Bucherer dolls are forgiven for some chips and damage. So
 desirable are these dolls that the adjustment would be only
 −20% to **−30%** depending on severity and location.
Mint, original or excellent condition...**+50%**

Composition and Papier-Mâché

Very light crazing .... **Acceptable**
Heavy crazing, cracking or peeling.. **−50%**
Small splits at corners of eye and/or mouth .... **−10%**
Heavy chipping to face .... **−75%**
Face repainted .... **−80%**

Redressed or undressed .... −25%

Mint and/or boxed .... +200% or more

Wax

Minor cracks or minor warp to head .... −20%

Major cracks or major warp to head .... −50%

Softening of features .... −20%

Rewaxed .... −70%

All original with sharp features and good color .... +200% or more

Celluloid

Cracks .... −80%

Discolored .... −70%

Mint .... +50%

Wood

Light crazing or minute paint touch-up .... Acceptable

Repainted head or heavy splits (depending on severity and
   location) .... −50% to −80%

Mint .... +100%

Plastic

Cracks or discoloration .... −75%

Hair combed .... −40%

Shelf dirt .... −10%

Redressed or missing accessories .... −50%

1950s, mint, boxed .... +200%*

1960s, mint, boxed .... +150%*

1970s, mint, boxed .... +50%*

1980s, mint, boxed .... +10%

1990s, mint, boxed .... List Value

*Or more, depending on the desirability of the doll

Selling a Doll

by Dawn Herlocher

You have decided to sell your doll. Now what do you do? Finding a new home for your doll may be somewhat challenging, and receiving a top selling price may be extremely difficult. Of course you want your doll to go to someone who will appreciate it, but it is equally important to be a confident, informed seller.

Identify Your Doll and Determine Its Condition

The first step in selling your doll is to accurately identify it. The books *200 Years of Dolls* or *Antique Trader's Doll Makers and Marks* are both comprehensive guides that are user-friendly.

The next step may be the hardest but most essential process— to accurately evaluate your doll's condition. No matter how much you love it, no matter how beautiful it is, or how close you were to the dear aunt who gave you this wonderful doll, if the doll is damaged or in less than great condition, do not expect to get "book" value for it. Refer to the price adjustment information on page 18-19 for help.

Before presenting your doll to any prospective buyer, you should take the time to pamper it a little. Remember the old saying, "eye appeal is buy appeal." Most patrons are willing to pay a little more for a doll that is in display condition.

Selling Options

Auction House or Dealer ♦ If you have an extremely rare and valuable doll, a reputable doll dealer or specialized auction house may be your best outlet. If the doll is truly desirable, an experienced dealer will want your doll so desperately that he or she will be anxious to pay top dollar to have it. Of course the dealer will want to make a profit when he or she sells the doll, but just being able to have a rare doll in inventory will make the doll almost irresistible.

The same holds true for any of the principal auction houses that specialize in selling dolls. Negotiate with the auctioneer for a reduced retention rate. A rare and desirable doll will be an advertising draw for the auction house, therefore, they should be happy to offer you a lower selling fee. Naturally, your bargaining powers will be dramatically reduced if your doll is damaged. Keep in mind that if you give a doll to an auction house, you may have no control over the final selling price. (*Note: See Antique Trader's Doll Makers & Marks* for addresses and phone numbers of auction houses specializing in dolls.)

Doll Club ◆ Selling your doll through a local doll club is always a good alternative. Doll collectors belong to doll clubs, and who better to offer a doll to than a collector? You have two choices: Either set an asking price, or suggest the club hold a silent auction for the doll. In either case you will have to make a donation to the club.

Advertisements ◆ Advertise your doll in one or more of the many excellent trade papers, such as *Antique Trader* or *Collectors United*. In addition to a limited number of collectors, the majority of trade subscribers are dealers, flea marketers, and e-Bay users. This is exactly the market you want to attract, but it may also be a less profitable group.

Classified ads in local newspapers or auction halls also have advantages. You will not have to transport or ship your doll; most likely your selling fees will be less; and more importantly, a very common or damaged doll will almost always command a higher price.

Shows & Flea Markets ♦ If you have a collection of dolls, you may want to try retailing them at a show or flea market. This will involve reserving a location at the show, pricing each doll, packing them for the move, and displaying them attractively once you're at the event. Check with the show promoter about available tables and table covers, lights, chairs or stools, loading, unloading, and parking. Shows require a lot of work, but you also will have fun meeting other doll collectors, and who knows—it could lead to a whole new career!

Internet ♦ Thousands of vendors have conducted successful transactions selling their collectibles via the Internet or e-Bay. If you opt to sell your doll this way, you must prepare photos of it along with a detailed description. You will most likely spend additional time everyday answering e-mail questions. Keep track of the under bidder throughout the transaction. Occasionally the high bidder fails to honor his or her obligation; contacting the under bidder may salvage a sale. Make sure that you request adequate shipping charges and allow sufficient time for any checks to clear the bank. Package your doll for safe shipping. Fill the inside of the head with tissue paper, if possible, to keep the eyes from jarring loose. Wrap the entire doll in bubble wrap; surround it with Styrofoam peanuts; and double box it. Always insure your package, even if your buyer neglects to do so.

Each of these selling opportunities has advantages and disadvantages. All will extract a fee for selling. Take the time and expense of shipping into consideration. If you are not satisfied with the results of one method, try another. Be courteous to any potential customer. And be patient—someone somewhere is waiting to own a wonderful doll just like the one you're selling.

10 Notable Doll Companies

by Dawn Herlocher

What determines a notable doll manufacturer? Is it the longevity of a company; the rarity of a particular doll; product innovation; collectible value; diversity of goods; the age of a doll; or perhaps its beauty? Or is it a combination of some or all of these characteristics?

"Notable" is a subjective term. Nevertheless, in my humble opinion, following is a list of what I consider the 10 most notable doll companies, with a brief explanation why. Your list of 10 notables may be different from mine but be just as acceptable.

In addition to this most notable list is my "Honorable Mention" list. Companies that have been instrumental, influential, and important in one way or another to the doll industry: Door of Hope; Joel Ellis; Gebrüder Heubach; Käthe Kruse; A. Marque; Morimura Brothers; Pleasant Company; Raggedy Ann and Andy; Société Française de Fabrication de Bébés & Jouets; A. Schoenhut & Company; W. P. A.; and Wilson Novelty Company.

Aetna Doll Company

In 1909 this small rather unremarkable Brooklyn, New York, doll company changed doll making history. A few years earlier, Solomon Hoffmann, a Russian immigrant, obtained the patent for "Can't Break Em" dolls. Doll manufacturers showed little interest in Hoffmann's formula, save for one, Aetna. Aetna purchased The First American Doll Factory from Hoffmann, along with the secret process for making composition doll heads. Shortly after the acquisition, Aetna entered a binding contract with E. I. Horsman Company, which eventually led to a merger, with Horsman securing the rights to Hoffmann's secret formula. Horsman's keen sense of marketing helped to promote composition dolls, but it was Aetna's foresight in obtaining the formula that was the catalyst for progress.

25" composition Aetna Mama Baby with cloth body, marked "EIH ©A. D. Co." $800

Alexander Doll Company

In 1923 Beatrice Alexander convinced her three sisters to help her make cloth dolls to sell in their parents' doll hospital. Beatrice's ambition and hard work led to the formation of her company, which produced not only cloth, but later composition, hard plastic, vinyl and most recently a line of limited edition porcelain dolls. Both the veteran collector and the doll novice are familiar with the attention to detail and character presentation given to each of the more than 7,000 high quality personality dolls introduced. It was the inspired genius of one woman that led to the celebrity status given to Madame Alexander dolls.

15" Sonja Henie by Madame Alexander, marked "Madame Alexander Sonja Henie" on head, all composition, open mouth with teeth, redressed in black skating attire and skates. "As is" condition. .... **$200-$250**

China Heads

Several manufacturers produced china head dolls continuously from circa 1840 to the present. The prolonged existence of the china head doll would seem to be ample justification for its inclusion of the top 10, but there is another. China head dolls may not be the most beautiful, nor most actively sought; however, they were the very first successfully mass-produced doll; after all, there is only ever one first. The enthusiastic reception given the early china head dolls encouraged hundreds of German doll companies to produce not only the untinted glazed china heads, but to progress to the tinted, unglazed bisque head dolls that fueled the European commerce for half a century.

16" German KPM china lady with molded bun (Krister Porzellan Manufaktur AG, Bavaria, founded 1831). With dark brown painted hair pulled back in bun with exposed ears. Pale blue eyes. On an early cloth body wearing a two-piece hand-sewn red cotton dress and a newer black velvet cape. Some light speckling to face. Body is sturdy with some soiling and wear, especially to toes. Very light scuffing on back of bun. .... **$4,000-$5,500**

Effanbee

Responsible for many significant innovations, beginning in 1910 and continuing until today, this prolific doll company has proven to be a creative pioneer in the American doll industry. The first realistically proportioned doll designed to resemble a real child, Patsy was also the first to have companion dolls, a special wardrobe, and her very own fan club. Effanbee's modernistic image was further enhanced with the 1934 introduction of "Dy-Dee," the first domestic drink and wet doll. While maintaining its commitment of excellence in the play doll market, Effanbee became a leader in the collector doll craze. Enlisting talented doll artists, initiating the Limited Edition Doll Club, and producing realistic celebrity and personality dolls, Effanbee has secured its position of excellence for future generations of doll collectors.

PATSY
Left, **9 1/2" composition Patsyette,** molded and painted hair and eyes, jointed, wearing original dress and shoes. .... **$450-$550**

Right, **6" composition Wee Patsy,** molded hair, painted eyes, jointed, painted socks and shoes, redressed, otherwise mint. .... **$450-$475**

Jumeau

Many will debate the inclusion of Jumeau and the exclusion of Bru, Steiner, Gaultier, and Mothereau among other extraordinary French doll manufacturers, however, it is the totality of Jumeau's ingenuity that dictates its inclusion. During the nearly 60 years prior to joining the Société Française de Fabrication de Bébés & Jouets in 1899, Jumeau produced magnificent bébés and fashionably attired poupée de mode (French fashion-type dolls) presenting a perfect example of the beauty and splendor of Parisian life. It is the fantastic, incredibly expressive character dolls such as the mischievous child; a laughing adolescent; the gorgeously sculptured heart-shaped face lady; and unbelievably sensitive worry-worn, ebony African woman that has set Jumeau apart from the other French doll manufacturers.

PORTRAIT JUMEAU BÉBÉ
13" second series portrait Jumeau Bébé. Brown paperweight eyes, wearing her original pale green silk outfit. Original French mohair wig, wire-frame lace hat and original spring in head. On a straight-wrist, eight-ball-jointed Jumeau body (minor wear and paint loss to fingers). Lacking shoes.
.... **$8,500-$9,000**

Kestner

The doll industry was the backbone of the German economy, and J. D. Kestner was head of the industry. Kestner began his career making papier-mâché notebooks; he quickly extended his talents to produce toys and dolls. Kestner participated in the 1840 Leipzig Fair as the first toymaker of Waltershausen, an impressive claim considering the toy capital that area was to become. Kestner was so successful that he employed over three-quarters of the total population in and around Waltershausen. The repertoire of Kestner dolls is impressive, including open- and closed-mouth dolly-faced dolls; chubby-faced babies; stylish Gibson ladies; cunning children, plus a wide range of character dolls. Often nicknames are used to promote a company or an individual; "King Kestner" was a title obviously earned by the Kestner industrial empire.

BISQUE DOME HEAD
24" Kestner bisque dome head, marked "JDK Made in Germany," blue sleep eyes, fully jointed composition body, wearing a white cotton baby dress and bonnet.
.... **$2,200-$2,400**

Mattel

Including Mattel was an almost painful experience. When so many really wonderful German and French antique doll manufacturers had to be excluded, to list Mattel as one the top 10 seems inconceivable. However, one word can explain the significance of Mattel, and that one word is Barbie (Barbara Millicent Roberts, like Cher and Elvis, needs only a first name, "Barbie"). You may or may not be a Barbie fan, but few can dispute the impact that she has had on the doll world. Barbie has been so successful that a third generation of children is now playing with her and her "A list" of friends. Barbie is so popular that Mattel is the world's largest manufacturer of women's wear, solely of Barbie costumes. Barbie has become so collectible that not naming Mattel would be ridiculous.

PONYTAIL #1
Barbie doll Ponytail #1, 1959.
"Played with" condition
.... **$700-$900**
Good to very good condition .... **$3,000-$4,000**
If perfect ... **$9,000-$9,500**

Armand Marseille

It is hard to imagine a doll company more notable than Armand Marseille. From 1885 to 1930 Marseille was the largest supplier of bisque heads in the world, reportedly producing more than a thousand bisque doll heads a day. In addition to their own registered molds, Marseille supplied bisque heads to more than 25 other companies. Along with the more affordable AM 390, Queen Louise, or Floradora, any advanced collector would be excited to add the more elusive glass-eyed Fanny or intaglio-eyed character doll to her collection. Endurance; volume; affordability; appeal; idealism; charm; and even beauty are all synonymous with the name Armand Marseille.

CHARACTER BABY
15" bisque head character baby, marked "Germany 971 A #4 M DRGM," brown stationary eyes, open mouth with teeth, jointed composition baby body, wearing an off-white dotted cotton dress and bonnet with blue ribbon.
.... **$650-$700**

Munich Art Dolls

Marion Kaulitz, originator of Munich Art Dolls, led the 1909 Puppen Reform – a movement in Bavaria towards the creation of realism in dolls. A review of Marion Kaulitz in *Studio Talk* is quoted: "When the artistic conscience began to invade the doll industry it fell to some artists of Dresden and Munich to introduce the change." The Munich Art Doll attracted a great deal of commercial attention, undoubtedly inspiring the leading doll manufacturers to copy the character doll trend. Munich Art Dolls are admired not only for their appealing avant-garde naturalism, but also for their historically significant contribution to the evolution of doll making.

17" all-original Munich Art Doll, modeled by Paul Vogelsanger. Photo courtesy Ellen Schroy **$8,700**

Simon & Halbig

The German porcelain factory of Wilham Simon and Carl Halbig began producing dolls heads sometime during the late 1860s. The earliest delicately decorated tinted and untinted bisque shoulder heads are typical of the remarkable number of fine quality dolls produced. Simon & Halbig patented several innovations, including lever-operated eyes; movable eyelids; eyelashes made of thread, and neck socket glazing. The fine quality bisque coupled with the artistically applied decoration resulted in Simon & Halbig obtaining an extremely impressive patron list, supplying bisque heads to several leading German manufacturers, in addition to being one of the very select few that supplied heads to the French market. It is the corporate associations enjoyed by Simon & Halbig that make the company, in my opinion, one of the most notable.

SIMON & HALBIG
20" Simon & Halbig, marked "S 15 H 949," open mouth with teeth, blue eyes, fully jointed composition body, redressed wearing a purple silk dress, new shoes. .... **$2,200-$2,600**

How to Use This Book

Warman's Dolls Field Guide is organized by the material used to make dolls. This allows readers to quickly focus their search for information because dolls are often categorized by the material used to make the head. There are separate sections on dolls made of all bisque, cloth, composition, metal, papier-mâché and wax, porcelain (including bisque heads, china heads, and parian), synthetic materials (celluloid, hard plastic, latex, rubber, and vinyl), and wood, as well as sections on automata and artist dolls. Each of those sections is then organized alphabetically by maker or style. At the back of the book you'll find a helpful glossary of doll terms and an index.

All Bisque Dolls

Bisque, china, parian, and porcelain are all forms of ceramics derived from a clay-based material to which feldspar and flint have been added. This mixture is molded, fired, painted, and fired again. Quality can range from the finest porcelain with beautifully detailed decoration to coarse and crudely painted "stone bisque." Factors determining a doll's quality include: the texture of the porcelain, the artistry applied in decorating the piece, the subject model, and the presence or absence of a glaze.

All bisque types include French, German, Japanese, bathing dolls, character babies, Frozen Charlotte, etc.

PIANO BABIES
These two unmarked German piano babies were intended for a child's instrument, such as a Schoenhut piano. The seated figure is about 3" tall. .... **$175-$225**

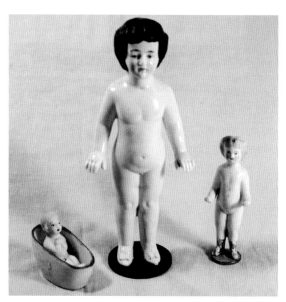

FROZEN CHARLOTTES

Though most Frozen Charlottes are standing figures with arms extended, some collectors also include tiny infants, like the one seen here in its bath, in this category. The middle doll is about 7" tall. Note the molded shoes on the two standing dolls.

Japanese baby in bathtub...$60-$70
7" Frozen Charlotte .... $245-$275
Smaller Charlotte with gold boots .... $325-$350

ALL BISQUE GROUP

From left: **5″** all bisque boy, jointed at shoulder and hip, brown glass eyes, brown hair, open mouth with teeth, painted stockings and shoes, wearing a brown suit. .... **$350-$400**

5 1/2″ all bisque, jointed at shoulder and hip, marked "104 5 1/2" on head, brown glass eyes, closed mouth, painted shoes and socks, blonde wig, wearing a cream-colored dress. .... **$375-$425**

4 1/2″ all bisque, marked "German" on back, molded blonde hair, painted side-glancing eyes, all jointed, painted shoes and socks, wearing a lace dress. .... **$200-$225**

4 1/2″ all bisque, marked "5701 Made in Germany," blue glass eyes, closed mouth (slight repair on back), all jointed, red hair, painted shoes and socks. "As is" condition. .... **$200-$225**

4 1/2″ all bisque, marked "3 Made in Germany," brown glass eyes, closed mouth, black wig, painted shoes and socks, wearing a violet lace dress. .... **$400-$450**

ALL BISQUE GROUP

From left: 5" all bisque, jointed, marked "Made in Germany," blonde wig, brown sleep eyes, open/closed mouth, painted shoes and socks, wearing a white lace dress. .... **$425-$475**

4" all bisque, jointed, marked with a bell and "367 10" (possibly made by C. F. Kling & Co., 1836 to 1941), blue stationary eyes, brown wig, painted shoes and socks. .... **$450-$475**

4" all bisque, marked "809 500 Germany," arms jointed at shoulders, painted blue eyes, closed mouth, blonde wig, painted shoes and socks, wearing a white dress with blue bonnet. .... **$250-$300**

4 1/2" all bisque, marked "Made in Germany," brown painted eyes, closed mouth, painted shoes and socks, wearing a white dress. .... **$250-$300**

2 1/4" all bisque jointed baby, marked "Germany," painted eyes and molded hair, wearing a white dress. .... **$100-$150**

3" all bisque jointed baby, marked "Germany," painted eyes and molded hair, wearing a white dress. .... **$200-$250**

BATHING BEAUTIES

Pair of bisque German bathing beauties: First is 6" bather with wig, in a recumbent pose holding her hands (tip of pinkie broken). Second is a 3 1/2" bather with molded hair, suit and cap. Larger figure has some distress to original knit bathing suit. .... **$750-$850/pair**

DOLLY NIPPON
4"-6" all bisque Japan "Dolly Nippon." Courtesy of McMasters-Harris
Auction
4" .... $100-$110
6" .... $125-$145

Artist Dolls

Though some collectors think of artist dolls as simply pretty statues, others consider them to be individually designed, crafted, produced works of art. Many of the artists are members of either the National Institute of American Doll Artists (N.I.A.D.A.) or Original Doll Artists Council of America (O.D.A.C.A.). Material, workmanship, subject matter, and visual or decorative appeal are all part of each doll's collectibility.

For more information on makers belonging to these two organizations, visit their Web sites at www.niada.org and www.odaca.org.

KATHY REDMOND HEADS
Two Kathy Redmond heads. French dame with elaborate hairdo, fancy full hat and numerous ribbons on rear of head; elderly lady. Overall fine condition.
French dame.. $600-$750
Elderly lady.. $350-$400

LEWIS SORENSEN ST. NICHOLAS
24" Lewis Sorensen wax St. Nicholas. Holding accessories in his hands and
a Christmas tree on his back. Blue inset glass eyes with a well-defined and
detailed face. Very good original condition. ....$1,600-$1,750

LEWIS SORENSEN GIBSON GIRL
24" Lewis Sorensen wax Gibson Girl. Beautiful detailed and sculpted face, lovely period costume. Excellent condition. From the collection of Julia Burke. Courtesy of Julia Burke, www.juliaburke.com.
....**$1,200-$1,400**

P.D. SMITH CHARACTER CHILD
22" P.D. Smith composition character child. Flirty glass eyes, open/closed
smiling mouth. Original costume. Courtesy of McMasters-Harris Auction.
.... **$3,200-$4,000**

MARTHA THOMPSON GEORGE AND MARTHA WASHINGTON
Two Martha Thompson dolls, dressed as George and Martha Washington.
All original and in excellent condition. .... **$2,500-$3,000/pair**

**MARTHA THOMPSON
QUEEN ELIZABETH II**
21" Martha Thompson
"Queen Elizabeth II"
(Martha Thompson, born
Huntsville, Ala., 1903, died
1964). With curls to rear and
exposed ears, wearing a tiara
with encrusted jewels. Molded necklace and cream-colored lace dress. All original
and in excellent condition.
.... **$1,500-$2,000**

EUNICE TUTTLE MARGUERITA
3 3/4" infant Marguerita by Eunice Tuttle. Jointed porcelain artist doll of baby Marguerita in its original box. Fine condition. .... **$600-$750**

EUNICE TUTTLE GIRL
4 1/2" jointed girl with doll by Eunice Tuttle. Jointed all-bisque artist doll of a girl holding her doll and standing in front of a table, contained in a Plexiglas cube. Fine condition. .... $900-$1,000

Automata

The term "automata" covers a range of mechanical figures.

Made around the world, mechanical dolls are evaluated based on costuming, condition, visual appeal, and intricacy of movement. Generally, value increases in direct relation to the doll's complexity. The more intricate the movements and the greater their number, the more valuable the automata. Working condition is important because repairs can be costly.

Well-known manufacturers of automatons—usually operated by spring-driven works—include Rousselot, Phalibois, Vichy, Fleischmann and Blodel, Lambert, and Roulette de Camp. Marks may be found on keys or on the inside of the housings. Doll heads were supplied by various doll manufacturers and were marked accordingly.

Animated dolls were first introduced in Germany and share some similarities with automatons. The spring clockwork of the automata is replaced by a rotating mechanism; turning a crank causes the figure to move, usually in a stiff and awkward style. Generally, the value of these dolls is determined more by charm and visual appeal than from the complexity of their movements.

Autoperipatetikos employ a clockwork mechanism within a walking body. Most are about 10 inches tall and may have patent marks.

Cymbalers contain a pressure-activated bellows mechanism within their bodies. When compressed, the arms come together. Heads are usually made of bisque and commonly resemble a baby or clown.

Walking, kicking, crying, and talking dolls were known as gigoteur. First patented in 1855 by Jules Steiner, the doll's body houses a flywheel regulator and clockwork mechanism. These dolls are typically marked "1," "2," "3," or are unmarked.

Marottes from France and Germany fall somewhere between a doll and a toy. They incorporate music boxes and whirling figures, and are decorated to represent a variety of characters from clowns to animals.

Swimming dolls, also known as Ondines, were once advertised as "Parisian Mechanician for Adult Amusement." They were made with either bisque or celluloid heads and cork bodies, with jointed wooden arms and legs that simulated swimming when wound by a key.

Early walking and talking dolls are often found with chain mechanisms. Others have wire arrangements connecting the arms and feet, a technique first used by Schoenhut wooden dolls. The talking device in early talking dolls consists of a bellows in the body that was activated by pulling strings, exerting pressure, or moving some part of the body. Some collectors also include phonograph dolls in this category.

BOY AND GIRL AUTOMATONS
French schoolboy and Fifi O'Toole automatons manufactured by Roulette Decamp, each 12" tall. Boy with schoolbag and a young girl holding an infant. When wound, they sway from left to right while also turning their heads. In very fine all original condition, boy's mechanism is sticky, probably in need of light lubrication. .... **$2,800-$3,500/pair**

GIRL WITH MIRROR AUTOMATON
French Lambert automaton of girl with mirror and powder puff (9" by
12 1/2" by 18"). A closed-mouth Tete Jumeau #5 with blue paperweight
eyes and bisque lower arms standing at a dressing table with mirror. When
activated, the doll turns her head from left to right, occasionally lowering
her head and powdering her nose. She then turns to the left to glimpse at
herself in the mirror held in her left hand. Clothing (probably not original)
in fragile condition. Some trim missing from base. Two tunes play when
activated. Worn condition..**$4,500-$6,000**

MOZART AUTOMATON
French automaton "Mozart" (8 1/2" by 10" by 12"). Paper label attached to bottom, "Serenade de Schubert" and "Menuet de Mozart." Automaton has drawer that, when pulled open, activates the mechanism. The bisque head pianist proceeds to move his hands across the keys while raising and lowering his head and turning side to side. Pin attached to drawer that activates mechanism is missing. This is just a minor repair and should not detract from the value. ....$3,500-$4,000

GIRL WITH BOUQUET
Tete Jumeau automaton (6" by 6" by 16"). An open-mouth Tete Jumeau #2 with brown paperweight eyes. When activated, the girl raises her right hand to smell her flowers while her head nods and left arm moves. Clothing and wig are older replacements, rub to end of nose. Various movements are inoperative. "As is" condition. .... **$900-$1,300**

LADY WITH EGG AUTOMATON

French automaton of a lady with egg, 16" tall, base 4" by 4 1/2". When activated, she taps the egg with a cymbal and the top of the egg opens, revealing a glass-eyed monkey peeking out. The head has blue paperweight eyes and is made of bisque with a closed mouth, and marked "M1" on rear. Clothing is made of silk and, if not original, shows some age. Overall very fine and in working condition. ....**$4,000-$5,000**

PUNCH AUTOMATON
"Punch"-type figure with cymbals, 19" tall, base 5" square. Brown-eyed Tete Jumeau #4 automaton in original costume and wig, clapping her cymbals together while nodding her head from left to right. Costume is frail with significant fraying. Base has been re-covered in maroon velvet. Overall movements and music are fine. ....**$7,000-$8,500**

SMOKING AUTOMATON
French smoking automaton, 23" tall, base 6" square. When activated, music plays, the gentleman nods his head and also swivels from left to right while raising his right hand, which contains an ivory-type cigarette holder, to take a puff of his cigarette. Marked Tete Jumeau #2 on head with blue paperweight eyes and open mouth with original wig, hat, pants, and shoes (coat has been replaced). Overall very good condition. .... **$8,000-$10,000**

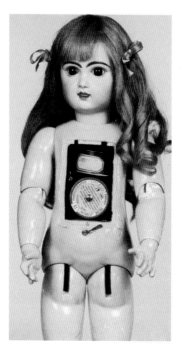

PHONOGRAPH DOLL
25" phonograph doll by Jumeau; bisque head, composition body; paperweight eyes, open mouth, Fait Dodo white wax cylinder. Courtesy of McMaster's Doll Auctions. .... **$9,000-$11,000**

Cloth Dolls

Many of the cloth dolls featured in this section were later mass-produced, after being created originally in the home by makers responding to families, friends, or just creative urges.

Martha Chase, circa 1889 to 1938

Made in Pawtucket, Rhode Island, Martha Chase dolls incorporated stockinet stretched over a mask with raised features. The head and limbs were sized with a coating of glue and paste, dried, and painted with oils. Ears and thumbs were applied separately. The earliest Chase dolls had pink sateen bodies. Later bodies were made from heavy, white cotton cloth stuffed with cotton batting.

Legs and arms were painted to above the knees and elbows, and an unstuffed area was left at each joint for ease of movement. Many of the Chase dolls were jointed at the shoulders, elbows, hips, and knees. Later dolls were jointed only at the hip and shoulders.

Chase was quoted in the 1917 issue of *Toys and Novelties*: "I first made the dolls about 28 years ago as an amusement and to see what I could do. For several years I did this and gave the dolls away to the neighborhood children. Then by chance a store buyer saw one and insisted upon my taking an order. That was about 20 years ago, and since then there has been a gradual increase in the business. The dolls gained recognition by their merits, as I have advertised them very little. Then someone who knew about them asked me to make one adult size to use in the hospital training schools, and from that has developed another new industry. Now we are making dolls that can be immersed in water and used in child welfare work."

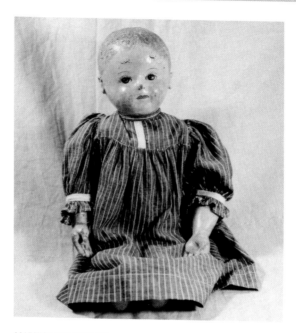

MARTHA CHASE BABY

16" Martha Chase baby weighted with sand. Ears and thumbs are stitched on, and head has a stitched pattern like that found on a softball. It shows the facial wear typical of these dolls.

Worn condition .... $300-$350

Good condition .... $800-$1,000

MARTHA CHASE HOSPITAL DOLL
21" Martha Chase "Hospital Doll." Some came with holes in the nostrils and ears for use in hospital training classes on the care of infants. Doll shows the facial wear typical of these dolls.
Very worn, redressed condition .... $350-$450
Good condition ....$1,000-$1,200

Effanbee Doll Co., founded circa 1910

Effanbee is an acronym for Fleischaker & Baum of New York. The company imported and distributed cloth display or souvenir dolls made in Spain by Klumpe. (Also see composition, synthetic.)

SPANISH DANCER
12" Klumpe Spanish Dancer holding baby. .... $125-$150

Folk Art Dolls

The term "folk art" is really one of perspective. The pieces that we now value as folk art often were not considered works of art by their makers. Rather, they had a form and function that were determined by the necessities of their day, or by the emotional investment in their creation. This is especially true of vintage folk art dolls.

When trying to determine the value of a folk doll, remember that folk art comes from a tradition outside of academic circles, and includes items both whimsical and utilitarian, whether elaborate or starkly simple. There are vast differences in the quality of folk dolls, depending on the talent and skill of the maker. Many are one-of-a-kind examples, and this makes general pricing difficult. The inventiveness and charm of a given doll can be more crucial factors than condition.

RAGGEDY ANN AND ANDY
Handmade 18" Raggedy Ann and Andy with button eyes, embroidered features, and yarn hair. Courtesy of McMasters-Harris Auction. .... **$2,000-$2,500**

TOPSY-TURVY
12" "Topsy-turvy" doll
(two half dolls joined
at the waist, one black
and one white), dates to the
late 1860s and comes with
homemade blanket. Hand-
painted features. Charming
and appealing doll in original
"loved" condition, complete
with blanket. Dolls with a
family history or detailed
provenance—or attributed to
a known maker—may bring
much more........**$700-$900**

Käthe Kruse, founded 1910

Based in Bavaria since the mid-1940s, vintage Käthe Kruse dolls were made of waterproof treated muslin, cotton, wool, and stockinette. The earliest dolls were marked in black, red, or purple ink on the bottom of the foot with the name "Käthe Kruse" and a three- to five-digit number. Celluloid dolls were also made in the late 1930s, and hard plastic in the early 1950s.

KÄTHE KRUSE ADULTS
Käthe Kruse adult figures, set of three. Two women, one bearded man. Some touchup to facial features of man, which has some flaking to paint. Overall soiling, water staining to man's costume and to the stockinette legs of the women. The rarity of these dolls allows forgiveness of their condition.
.... **$6,750-$7,500/set**

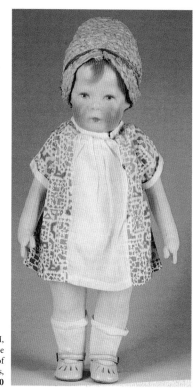

KÄTHE KRUSE CHILD
17" original later #I, signed Käthe Kruse child. Courtesy of James Julia Auctions, Inc....... $4,800-$5,200

Lenci, founded 1919

Established in Turin, Italy, Lenci felt dolls are the standard against which all similar dolls are measured. They were first created by Elena Konig Scavini and her brother, Bubine Konig.

Lenci was the first company to produce dolls using the pressed-felt method to give the faces dimensional character.

Lenci dolls are often referred to in series, such as "Mascotte" for the small 9" characters; "Hard Faced" for composition, mask, or flocked plastic heads; and "Bambino" for bent-limb babies. Code numbers are also commonly used; for example, children with hollow, felt torsos are in the 300 series, pouty-face dolls in the 1500 series, ladies or gentlemen in the 165 series, and girl dolls in the 700 series.

Lenci dolls may be marked with a hangtag, clothing label, or a purple or black "Lenci" stamp on the bottom of a foot. This stamp has a tendency to wear off.

LENCI MATADOR
14" Italian felt Lenci matador. All-original Lenci character with brown painted eyes. Some light soiling and fading of cheek color.
.... $1,100-$1,400

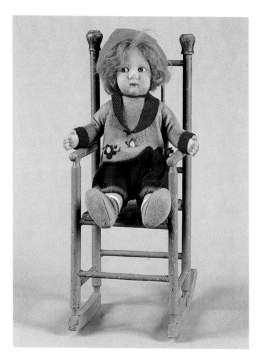

LENCI FELT DOLL
11" all original Lenci felt doll, movable limbs, in fair condition.
....$300-$500

LENCI FELT DOLL
11" well-loved Lenci felt doll, painted face, movable limbs, significant wear.
Poor, badly worn condition. ....$50-$75

LENCI BOUDOIR JESTER
28" Lenci boudoir jester doll, felt painted face, cloth body, white satin jester outfit with black felt dots, black satin hat and black felt shoes; all original and mint condition. ....$2,500-$3,000

Lenci-Type Dolls

Companies that produced copies of Lenci dolls include: Alma, Alpha, Alexander, American Stuffed Novelty, Amfelt, Averill, Chad Valley, Celia, Davis, Deans, Eros, Fiori, Giotti, La Rosa, Magis, Perotti, Pori, Raynal, and Wellings.

LENCI-TYPE DOLLS
Four 15" Lenci-type dolls, possibly Pori, all original, felt stuffed, jointed limbs, painted side-glancing eyes, each wearing clothing made of felt and organdy; all dolls in worn, "played with" condition. Third doll missing shoes and replaced socks. .... **$200-$250 each**

Pillow and Rag Doll Makers

Pillow or rag dolls were printed or lithographed, designed to be cut, sewn, and stuffed at home. Detailed instructions were printed alongside the figures. Many early printed dolls were produced in New England, the center of American textile manufacturing in the 1880s, and it was at this time that patented rag dolls appeared in great quantities in the United States.

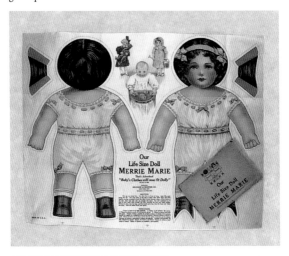

SELCHOW & RIGHTER MERRIE MARIE
22" Merrie Marie by Selchow & Righter, uncut cloth doll with original envelope. Pristine condition. .... **$500-$750**

Ravca Dolls, established 1930s

Ravca dolls were created by Bernard Ravca, originally of Paris. Ravca won first prize at the Paris Fair with his two life-sized figures of a Normandy peasant and his wife. Ravca came to the United States during World War II and became an American citizen in 1947.

RAVCA FRENCH COUPLE
18" Ravca silk sculptured man and woman, marked "Made in France," painted character faces, cloth bodies, sculptured hands; he carries a fish basket and she carries knitting, each with leather shoes. .... **$600-$750 each**

Sheppard & Co., Philadelphia Baby, circa 1900

Sheppard & Co.'s Philadelphia Baby, also known as the Sheppard Baby, were cloth dolls sold at the J. B. Sheppard Linen Store on Chestnut Street in Philadelphia. The designer, maker, and exact dates of manufacture are unknown.

PHILADELPHIA BABY
20" Philadelphia Baby with trunk and wardrobe. About six outfits, several pairs of shoes, four hats, and many undergarments/pajamas. Wear to face and head, old over-painting to doll. Clothing in very good original condition.

Good condition .... $8,000-$10,000
"As is" condition ....$2,000-$2,200
Trunk and extra clothing ....$2,500-$3,000

Steiff, founded circa 1880s

Margarete Steiff (1847-1909) was an accomplished seamstress, making women's and children's clothing out of wool felt. In 1880, she designed and created a small felt elephant pincushion. The creature's popularity prompted her to begin commercially producing small stuffed animals.

According to the Steiff Co., Margarete's nephew, Richard, designed a small, jointed, mohair bear that was exhibited at the 1903 Leipzig Toy Fair.

By coincidence, at about this same time, President Theodore Roosevelt traveled to Mississippi on a hunting expedition. One evening, a bear cub wandered into camp. Roosevelt refused to kill the young bear; instead he chased it back to its mother. The *Washington Post's* political cartoonist, Clifford Berryman, a member of the hunting party, drew a cartoon of the president chasing the bear. Thereafter, "Teddy's Bear" was in every cartoon Berryman did of Roosevelt. In 1906, at his daughter's wedding reception held at the White House, decorations were Steiff bears dressed as hunters and fishermen. In the next year, one million Steiff bears sold.

The Steiff factory operated for many years as a cottage industry. Women would pick up the raw materials at the factory and return with a finished toy.

Steiff markings have changed several times. In 1892, a camel was used, but never registered. In 1898, the elephant with his trunk forming the letter "S" was used, but again without being registered. The teddy bear, introduced as "Petz," was never registered, and competing firms were able to manufacture teddy bears.

An application by Steiff dated December 1904 seeks a register "for a button in the ear for toys of felt and similar material."

Margarete wrote to her customers to inform them: "...From November 1, 1904 on, each of my products, without exception, shall have as my trademark a small nickel button in the left ear."

Steiff also produced dolls advertised as "jovial lads and buxom maidens." They came with felt pressed heads with a seam down the middle of the face, mohair wigs, glass eyes, and large feet.

The features on authentic Steiff dolls are often hand painted and embroidered, and seams are frequently hand sewn, qualities missing from copies.

STEIFF HEDGEHOGS
Two 10" Steiff Hedgehogs, characters Mom (Micki) and Pop (Mecki), felt stuffed bodies, bur hair, faces are made of a rubberized molded material, all original clothing made of felt and cotton. ....$400-$600 each

STEIFF MARIONETTE
11" Steiff Marionette girl, felt stuff body, painted rubber-like face, yarn hair, felt dress. .... $75-$125

STEIFF CHARACTERS
Left, **13" Steiff character farmer** with spade, felt body with fur hair and whiskers, pictured with his friend, **Lucky**; both have rubber-like molded faces, felt clothing, leather shoes, and original tags. ....**$300-$400 each**

STEIFF FARMER AND WIFE
18" Steiff farmer (#9112/45) and **farmer's wife** (#9110/43), stuffed felt with ear buttons, painted faces, felt and cotton clothes, leather shoes, all original. ....**$250-$350 each**

W.P.A. Dolls, 1930s

Made in the United States during the 1930s as part of Franklin D. Roosevelt's New Deal, the Works Progress Administration provided work for artists and seamstresses struggling during the Great Depression. Cloth dolls were created representing characters from fairy tales and folklore, and historical figures from both the United States and various foreign countries.

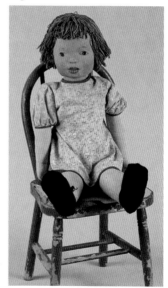

W.P.A.
22 1/2" W.P.A. doll made in Milwaukee, string hair, cloth body rigidly stuffed. The *Milwaukee Journal* photographed Eleanor Roosevelt holding this doll, adding greatly to the doll's appeal.
.... **$1,800-$2,400**

Izannah Walker, mid-19th century

Izannah Walker of Central Falls, Rhode Island, made dolls with heavily oil-painted features on slightly sculptured faces.

In June 1873, Walker applied for a patent for her "rag dolls." According to patent law, it was illegal for her to have made her dolls for more than two years prior to her application date. There are reports, however, that Walker was making and selling dolls as early as the 1840s.

The patent application described layering and pressing cloth treated with glue in a heated two-part mold. The body was then sewn, stuffed, and glued around a wooden armature. Hands and feet were hand sewn. The entire doll was then hand painted in oil colors. The hair was painted with corkscrew curls or short and straight. Other characteristics include applied molded ears, stitched fingers, and either bare feet with stitched toes or painted-on high-laced shoes.

An Izannah Walker doll in very good condition is incredibly rare.

IZANNAH WALKER CLOTH DOLL
18" cloth Izannah Walker doll. Painted ringlets in front of ears and going around head. Brown painted eyes. Dressed in brown floral cotton with red wool slip and muslin underwear, red cotton poke bonnet. Comes with early patchwork quilt. Normal wear on face and neck with more wear to back of head. Nose has been repaired, and hands and arms are repainted. Later molded ears. Much wear to her lower legs and feet with repairs to the ankles, tips of the toes are open exposing horsehair stuffing.
....$9,000-$10,000

OTHER CLOTH DOLLS

GEORGENE NOVELTIES BELOVED BELINDY
15" Georgene Novelties Beloved Belindy in mint condition with original
box. Courtesy of McMasters-Harris Auction.............................**$3,800-$4,200**

HEDGEHOG MUSICIANS
4" **hedgehog musicians** (Peter Max?) wearing red stocking caps.
....$200-$225

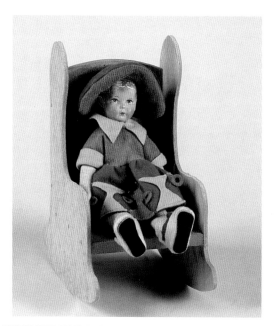

CLOTH OVER MASK FACE DOLL
9" cloth over mask face (similar to Nora Wellings), painted eyes, all original felt clothing and shoes. Worn condition...**$75-$125**

CLOTH DOLL GROUP
From left: **9" silk mask face,** cloth body, all original, wool embroidered.
....$175-$200
6 1/2" silk mask face, tagged "Capri Treasures of Florence, Italy," all original. .... $75-$125
6 1/2" silk mask face, made in Italy, hair braided on sides around ears, all original. ....$75-$125
6 1/2" silk mask face, marked "Florence, Italy," cloth body, arms are plastic or celluloid, hair is braided in a bun in back, all original. .... $75-$125

KÄTHE KRUSE-TYPE
10" painted cloth face (Käthe Kruse-type), cloth, hard-stuffed jointed body,
wearing original felt green outfit and felt shoes. "Played with" condition.
....$200-$225

Composition Dolls

Often called "compo" by collectors, composition is a generic term to describe a type of doll, popular in the first half of the 20th century, made of a pulp-based mixture of sawdust and glue that is molded, processed, and painted.

The painted surface of the composition heads tends to craze and is susceptible to damage caused by environmental extremes. Heat, dampness, and temperature changes quickly take their toll. In general, collectors accept slight crazing as a matter of course for composition dolls. If badly crazed, cracked, peeling, or repainted, values can be reduced considerably.

Composition dolls were made by countless manufacturers in various countries, and many are unmarked.

COMPOSITION DOLL MAKERS

Alexander Doll Co. (Madame Alexander), founded 1923

A true American success story, the Alexander Doll Co. was established by the Alexander sisters—Beatrice Alexander Behman, Rose Alexander Schrecking, Florence Alexander Rapport, and Jean Alexander Disick. Their parents, Russian immigrants Maurice and Hannah Alexander, owned and operated the first doll hospital in the United States.

The first Alexander dolls were made of cloth. In 1929, a line of dolls appeared in trade catalogs advertised as "Madame Alexander." The following year, the Alexander sisters expanded this line, now commonly known as "Madame Alexander Dolls." (Also see synthetic.)

Madame Alexander Dolls include more than 7,000 different personalities identified by their costumes or wrist tags.

In 1995 the company was acquired by The Kalzen Breakthrough Partnership, a private capital fund.

MADAME ALEXANDER STORYBOOK (TINY BETTY)
Two 7" composition Madame Alexander storybook (Tiny Betty) dolls, painted eyes to the side, painted shoes and socks, blonde mohair wigs, original dresses, one marked "Am. Girl, Madame Alexander, NY, USA" and the other marked "Fairy Princess, Madame Alexander."
....$300-$400 each

MADAME ALEXANDER LITTLE GENIUS
22" Madame Alexander character baby, ("Little Genius" or "McGuffey"?),
marked "Alexander" on head, composition head and limbs, cloth body,
brown hair and sleep eyes, wearing a pink and white dress. This doll appears
redressed in "played with" condition .... **$200-$300**

MADAME ALEXANDER PINKY
15" Madame Alexander "Pinky," composition head and limbs, sleep eyes, molded hair, cloth body, wearing original net-type dress and bonnet, missing shoes. .... $250-$300

MADAME ALEXANDER WENDY
11" composition doll, marked "Madame Alexander," Wendy face, painted eyes and mouth, blonde wig, wearing an "Alice in Wonderland" outfit, replaced shoes. "As is" condition. .... $75-$125

MADAME ALEXANDER 17"
17" composition, marked "Madame Alexander," jointed body, blue sleep eyes, open mouth with teeth, brown human-hair wig, wearing a white organdy dress, replaced clothing. .... **$300-$400**

MADAME ALEXANDER BABY
23" composition baby, marked "Madame Alexander," blue sleep eyes, closed mouth, cloth body and composition limbs, wearing a pink and white sweater dress and bonnet, replaced clothing. .... $200-$250

MADAME ALEXANDER DIONNE QUINTUPLET 11 1/2" **Madame Alexander Dionne Quintuplet doll,** marked on head, brown sleep eyes, all composition toddler body, brown hair, wearing original pink organdy dress, shoes appear replaced. ....$300-$350

MADAME ALEXANDER DIONNE QUINTUPLETS
Set of 7 1/2" Dionne Quintuplet babies, all marked "Dionne" on heads and "Madame Alexander" on backs, all composition jointed bodies, wearing respective colors (Yvonne, pink; Annette, yellow; Cecile, green; Emelie, lavender; Marie, blue), wear and crazing. "As is" condition. .... **$1,000-$1,500**

MADAME ALEXANDER DIONNE QUINTUPLETS
Set of 16" Madame Alexander Dionne Quintuplets, marked on heads, "Madame Alexander Dionne," molded hair, brown sleep eyes, composition heads, shoulder plates and limbs on cloth bodies, in identical white dresses, three missing bibs... **$1,800-$2,400**

DIONNE QUINTUPLET
17" Madame Alexander Dionne Quintuplet doll, head marked "Dionne Alexander," back marked "Alexander," brown sleep eyes, closed mouth, all composition jointed toddler body, wearing pink organdy dress and bonnet with tag marked, "Genuine Dionne Quintuplet Dolls, Madame Alexander"; appears in original and good condition. .... **$700-$900**

MADAME ALEXANDER DIONNE QUINTUPLET
9 1/2" Madame Alexander Dionne Quintuplet toddler doll, marked "Dionne, Alexander" on head and back, all composition jointed body, human-hair wig over plain head, open mouth, sleep eyes, wearing original pink dress and bonnet. .... $400-$600

MADAME ALEXANDER SONJA HENIE

18" Sonja Henie by Madame Alexander, all composition, brown sleep eyes, open mouth with teeth, blonde wig, redressed in aqua taffeta, white marabou, skates. "As is" condition. ... **$400-$600**

American Character Doll Co., 1919 to 1968

Located in New York, 16 styles of composition dolls were made with the trade name Aceedeecee – "ACDC" for American Character Doll Co.

The first dolls marketed by American Character were composition bent-limb babies with cloth bodies. By 1923, the trade name "Petite" was adopted.

AMERICAN CHARACTER BABY
15" American Character baby, composition head and limbs, blue sleep eyes, cloth body, molded hair, redressed in a long white ruffled dress. .. **$300-$325**

Arranbee Doll Co., 1922 to 1959

Founded in New York, Arranbee Doll Co. imported dolls, heads, and parts, and later manufactured its own doll heads. Vogue Doll Co. acquired Arranbee in 1959 but continued to use the "R&B" mark until 1961. (Also see synthetic.)

ARRANBEE NANCY
17" composition R&B Nancy. All-original composition girl with brown sleep eyes, wearing floor-length dress and bonnet. Excellent original condition. ....$1,000-$1,500

Arrow Novelty Co., founded 1920

Based in New York, Arrow Novelty Co. is best known for its Skookum Indian dolls designed by Mary McAboy of Missoula, Montana, and patented in 1914. Most early doll heads were made of clay and/or composition. Indian blankets were wrapped around wooden frames, leaving very little of the bodies to be seen. The dolls' costumes were made to represent various tribes, with sizes ranging from a few inches to several feet. Most are marked with a paper label on the foot that reads "Skookum Bully Good Indian."

ARROW NOVELTY CO. SKOOKUMS
15" Skookum squaw and papoose, two 11" squaws, 13" Skookum chief; clay-based faces with wigs, wool blankets, wood dowel feet and legs.
.... **$200-$300 each**

Berwick Doll Co., 1918 to 1925

This short-lived firm made the "Famlee" line of composition dolls, patented by David Wiener. They came boxed in a set that included a basic doll body, costumes, and several interchangeable heads.

BERWICK FAMLEE
Famlee doll with 14 different heads. Circa 1920s. With 14 of 16 possible heads, and comes with original paperwork and two outfits. Flaking to composition heads. "As is" condition, missing most costumes. .... **$500-$700/set**

George Borgfeldt & Co., 1881 to late 1950s

George Borgfeldt & Co., a New York importer, had exclusive North American rights to distribute dolls from several European manufacturers in addition to many prominent American companies.

Borgfeldt may be best remembered for promoting two dolls that have become icons of doll collecting: Grace Putnam's Bye-Lo Baby and Rose O'Neill's Kewpie.

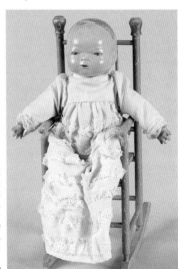

BORGFELDT BYE-LO 12" composition, marked "Grace Storey Putnam Bye-Lo" on head, cloth body, celluloid hands, blue sleep eyes, inappropriately dressed in white cotton and lace dress, wear to head. "As is" condition.
..........................**$75-$150**

Cameo Doll Co., 1922 to 1970

Located in Port Allegheny, Pennsylvania, founder and president Joseph Kallus gained recognition through his work with Rose O'Neill in the modeling of dolls she created, especially the Kewpies. Cameo Doll Co. became the sole manufacturer of composition Kewpies in the United States. George Borgfeldt & Co. distributed them along with other dolls by Cameo.

Many Cameo dolls are considered to be among the finest quality American dolls made in the 20th century.

It is common for early Cameo dolls to be unmarked or to have only a wrist tag. Later dolls were usually well marked and, after 1970, "S71" was added. In 1970, Cameo was acquired by the Strombecker Corp. of Chicago.

CAMEO GIGGLES
14" composition Giggles by Cameo, molded hair with bangs and bun in back (which has a hole through which to pull a ribbon), side-glancing eyes, Kewpie-style mouth, wearing a romper. Face and hair appear repainted, and the body is in poor condition. "As is" condition. .... $75-$125

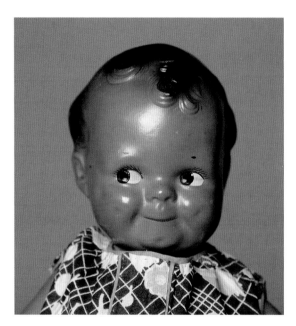

CAMEO SCOOTLES
13" black composition Scootles. Very good condition in old clothes and replaced shoes. Some peeling of paint on neck in back. .... **$700-$800**

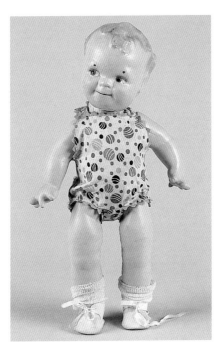

CAMEO SCOOTLES
16" composition Scootles by Cameo, painted eyes and molded hair, wearing a print romper; crazed but original condition. .... **$500-$700**
Mint condition.. .... **$1,200-$1,400**

CAMEO KEWPIE
11 1/2" composition Kewpie, jointed at shoulders, eyes painted to side, with heart label "Kewpie by Rose O'Neill," molded hair, painted mouth, wearing a red-dotted dress. Body appears badly crazed.................................. $200-$300

Effanbee Doll Co., founded circa 1910

Effanbee is an acronym for Fleischaker & Baum of New York. The firm's Patsy doll was the first realistically proportioned American-made doll designed to resemble a real child. She was also the first doll for which companion dolls were created, and the first to have a wardrobe and fan club. In 1934, Effanbee introduced "Dydee," the first drink-and-wet doll. The company also imported and distributed cloth display or souvenir dolls made in Spain by Klumpe. (Also see cloth, synthetic.)

EFFANBEE BOY AND GIRL
Left, **17 1/2" girl,** marked "Effanbee Dewee Design," painted blue eyes, closed mouth, composition body marked "Effanbee USA," wearing red coat and hat. Shoes and socks appear replaced..... **$2,500-$2,700**

Right, **18" boy,** marked "Effanbee Dewee Design," blond hair, painted eyes, closed mouth, wearing a tweed suit and cap. Shoes and socks appear replaced..... **$2,500-$2,700**

EFFANBEE AMISH FAMILY
11" and 7" Amish couple and child by Effanbee ("Baby Grumpy" molds), composition limbs, cloth bodies, mohair wigs, all original clothing in felt and cotton. In worn condition. ....$600-$800/set

EFFANBEE SWEETIE PIE AND PATSY
Left, **19" composition head and limbs Sweetie Pie,** flirty blue sleep eyes, brown hair, cloth body, appropriately redressed in white dress and sunbonnet, missing shoes. .... **$300-$350.**

Right, **14" composition Patsy doll,** brown sleep eyes, dark blonde wig, appropriately redressed in a lavender cotton dress and hat. .... **$600-$650**

EFFANBEE BIG BROTHER
16" Effanbee Big Brother, 1940s, painted eyes, string hair, cloth body, redressed, damaged hands. .... **$200-$250**

EFFANBEE CANDY KID
14" composition Effanbee Candy Kid, molded hair, blue sleep eyes, wearing red shorts and white shirt. "As is" condition.
.... $200-$250

**EFFANBEE
LITTLE LADY**
17 1/2" composition head,
marked "Effanbee, Little
Lady," composition body,
blue sleep eyes, closed
mouth, dark hair, wearing
original red, white, and
blue outfit, replaced shoes.
Appears in good condi-
tion. .... $350-$400

**EFFANBEE
ANN SHIRLEY**
21 1/2" composition,
marked "Ann Shirley,"
brown sleep eyes, reddish
brown hair, redressed
in pink dress and shoes.
"Played with" condition.
.... $300-$350

**EFFANBEE
ANN SHIRLEY**
27" composition **Ann Shirley,** brown hair, blue sleep eyes, white blouse and black jumper, brown strap shoes; all original, good condition.
.... $700-$900

**EFFANBEE
ANN SHIRLEY**
**27" composition Ann
Shirley,** blonde hair, brown
sleep eyes, redressed in a
white dress and red strap
shoes; damaged toes.
.... **$250-$300**

EFFANBEE BABY TINYETTES AND PATSY
From left: **7" composition baby, marked "Effanbee Baby Tinyette,"** blue painted eyes, molded hair, redressed in white knit outfit, poor condition.
....$50-$75

10" composition marked "Effanbee Patsy Baby," blue sleep eyes, molded hair, painted mouth, probably original blue coat and hat. .... **$300-$400**

7 1/2" composition toddler, marked "Baby Tinyette," painted brown eyes, painted mouth, wearing blue dress, coat, and hat, appears in good condition... **$400-$450**

EFFANBEE PATSY BABYETTE
Left, **9" composition, marked "Patsy Baby,"** karakul wig, blue sleep eyes, closed mouth, redressed in pink dress and bonnet (not original). **$200-$300.** Right, **9 1/2" composition, marked "Effanbee,"** molded hair, cloth body, painted mouth, blue sleep eyes, wearing pink dress and bonnet, possibly original. .... **$300-$350**

EFFANBEE PATSYETTE & WEE PATSY

Left, **9 1/2" composition Patsyette,** molded and painted hair and eyes, jointed, wearing original dress and shoes. .... **$450-$550**

Right, **6" composition Wee Patsy,** molded hair, painted eyes, jointed, painted socks and shoes, redressed, otherwise mint. .... **$450-$475**

EFFANBEE PATSY, PATSYKIN
From left: **11" unmarked,** brown painted eyes, molded hair, painted closed mouth, wearing organdy dress and hat; "as is" condition. ....**$50-$75**

11" composition Patsykin, blue sleep eyes, painted mouth, brown hair, wearing blue and white dress (possibly original). .... **$550-$650**

14" composition, marked "Patsy PAT. PEND. DOLL," molded hair, painted brown eyes, redressed in dark teal coat, "as is" condition. .... **$200-$250**

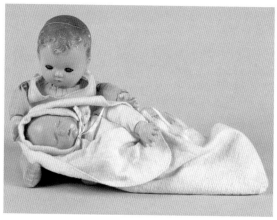

EFFANBEE PATSY BABY AND BABYETTE

Seated: **10" composition head,** marked "Effanbee Patsy baby" cloth body, composition hands, "as is" condition, undressed. ....$50-$75

Sleeping: **11" composition head,** marked "Babyette," with painted sleeping eyes, closed mouth, composition hands, cloth body, wearing pink layette. ....$300-$400

EFFANBEE PATRICIA
15" composition, marked
"Patricia," brown sleep
eyes, painted closed mouth,
wearing gold-colored coat
and hat; probably not
original. Doll appears to
be repainted.
Repainted and redressed
.............................$75-$150
Not repainted but re-
dressed .... $400-$500
Original good condition
.,,........................ $700-$900

EFFANBEE PATSY
14" composition head Patsy, blue painted eyes to the side, reddish molded hair, composition body, fair condition. **$400-$500**

EFFANBEE PATSY AND PATSY JR.

Left, **16" composition Patsy Joan marked "Effanbee Patsy,"** green sleep eyes, molded hair, composition body, redressed in coat and hat; doll mint.
....**$550-$650**

Right, **11" composition, marked "Effanbee Patsy Jr.,"** molded hair, composition body, redressed in green coat and hat. ....**$300-$400**

EFFANBEE PATSY ANN
19" composition, marked "Patsy Ann," green sleep eyes, molded hair, wearing a checked romper and sunbonnet; replaced shoes. .... **$600-$700**

EFFANBEE PATSY LOU
**22" composition, marked
"Patsy Lou,"** reddish
molded hair, green sleep
eyes, wearing a pink wool
coat and hat; replaced
shoes. Very good condi-
tion. .... $600-$700

**EFFANBEE
PATSY LOU**
**22" composition, marked
"Patsy Lou,"** brown sleep
eyes, molded hair under
wig, wearing a blue sailor
dress; replaced shoes; wig
in poor condition.
.... $300-$400

**EFFANBEE
BRIGHT EYES**
22" Bright Eyes, wig and
dress are in poor condi-
tion, but the doll appears
to be in good condition.
.... **$350-$450**

E.I. Horsman & Co., founded 1865

Edward Imeson Horsman founded this well-known doll company in New York. Beginning in the early 1900s, Horsman produced a variety of popular composition dolls. The dolls had painted hair or wigs, forward- or side-glancing, painted or sleep eyes, and open or closed mouths, with or without teeth. As time went on, even more variations were incorporated. Often, a doll was manufactured with a mix of characteristics, entirely different from the norm, or the same mold was given more than one name.

Around 1890, a Russian inventor, Solomon D. Hoffmann, brought his formula for "unbreakable" composition doll heads to America. Horsman eventually was able to secure the rights to Hoffmann's formula.

Horsman is famous for marketing the Billiken doll, originally created by Florence Pretz of Kansas City, Missouri. It is reported that during the first six months of production, Horsman sold more than 200,000 Billikens. (Also see synthetic.)

HORSMAN BILLIKEN
12" Billiken marked **"Horsman,"** composition head, teddy bear style body, label on chest illegible. Although in poor condition, he is rare and historically significant.
.... **$400-$500**

**HORSMAN
BRIGHT STAR**
14" Horsman "Bright Star," all composition, jointed body, all original in blue dress, white apron, straw hat, with original tag. Pristine condition.
.... $500-$750

HORSMAN JEANIE
14 1/2" composition by Horsman, marked "Jeanie Horsman" on back of head, cloth body, brown tin sleep eyes, molded hair, cotton dress. "As is" condition.. $200-$250

HORSMAN CHILD
20" composition child by Horsman, brown sleep eyes, open mouth with teeth, brown curls, all jointed, wearing a pink dress, replaced wig and costume............ **$175-$200**

HORSMAN JEANETTE MCDONALD
21" Jeanette McDonald by Horsman, all composition, open mouth, brown sleep eyes, blonde wig, some facial crazing, replaced dress and socks. Called a "slender child." "As is" condition. .... **$200-$300**

HORSMAN MAMA DOLL
24" composition, marked "Horsman Doll," blue sleep eyes, open mouth with teeth, blonde mohair wig, cloth body, redressed in a peach-colored cotton dress. ....**$200-$250**

Mary Hoyer Doll Manufacturing Co., 1925 to 1970s

Located in Reading, Pennsylvania, Mary Hoyer owned and operated a yarn shop, selling a wide variety of yarns and craft supplies through her mail-order business. She wanted a small, slim doll to use as a model for her clothing designs.

Hoyer enlisted the aid of Bernard Lipfert, a doll sculptor, to design a doll for her. The Fiberoid Doll Co. in New York produced the composition dolls until 1946, when hard plastic became available.

MARY HOYER GIRL
14" Mary Hoyer composition girl, marked in a circle on her back, "The Mary Hoyer Doll," blue sleep eyes, wearing a pink dress. Fair condition.
.... **$500-$550**

Ideal® Novelty and Toy Co., founded 1902

Morris Mitchom and A. Cohn founded Ideal initially to produce Mitchom's teddy bears.

Ideal was one of the few large companies that made its own composition dolls. American Character, Arranbee, Eugenia, and Mary Hoyer were among Ideal's customers. (Also see synthetic.)

IDEAL MAMA BABY
17" composition Mama Baby, marked "Ideal Doll" on head, cloth body, closed mouth. Appears original and in good condition.
.... **$350-$400**

IDEAL CHILD
21" composition child, marked "Ideal Doll USA," brown sleep eyes, brown hair, wearing original olive-green dress. Original but "played with" condition. .... $200-$300

IDEAL MAMA BABY
27" composition Mama Baby, marked "Ideal Made in USA" on head, reddish brown hair, sleep eyes, wearing yellow taffeta dress with ribbon lace trim and bows. (Unusual this size.) "Played with" condition. ...... **$300-$400**

**IDEAL
DEANNA DURBIN**
21" **Deanna Durbin,**
marked "Ideal" on back,
blue sleep eyes, open
mouth with teeth, white
cotton dress with green
dots may be original.
.... **$700-$900**

IDEAL SHIRLEY TEMPLE
12" composition Shirley Temple by Ideal, marked on head "11 Shirley Temple" and on back "Shirley Temple," with suit tag marked "Genuine Shirley Temple Doll, Ideal Toy Corp." Poor wig, face color faded, costume torn and faded, poor condition. .... **$200-$250**

**IDEAL
SHIRLEY TEMPLE**
**13" composition Shirley
Temple** by Ideal, marked
on head "Shirley Temple
Ideal Co.," and on back
"Shirley Temple 13," brown
sleep eyes, with net for
hair, hair restyled, wearing original "Baby Take
a Bow" dress with blue
dots and blue trim, and
replaced shoes.
.... $400-$500

**IDEAL
SHIRLEY TEMPLE
13" composition Shirley
Temple,** marked "Ideal
Genuine Shirley Temple,"
composition jointed body,
poor wig, faded face,
costume worn, labeled
"Genuine Shirley Temple,"
replaced shoes.
.... $200-$250

IDEAL SHIRLEY TEMPLE
17" composition Shirley Temple by Ideal, marked on head and back, appears in original good condition with moderate crazing, jointed body, blonde curly hair, wearing original blue and white dotted dress. **$500-$600**

**IDEAL
SHIRLEY TEMPLE
22" composition Shirley
Temple,** brown sleep eyes,
original wig, appears in
good clean condition with
nice bright face coloring,
redressed. .... **$700-$900**

IDEAL BABY SHIRLEY TEMPLE
18" composition Baby Shirley Temple, marked "Shirley Temple" on head, blue flirty eyes, molded hair, open mouth with teeth, wearing original clothes and shoes. ....**$1,400-$1,600**

OTHER COMPOSITION DOLLS

Three 7 1/2" Dionne Quints, unmarked, probably made in Japan, all composition jointed babies, painted eyes and mouths, molded hair, wearing organdy dresses, very appealing, good condition. ....$175-$250 each

8" composition shoulder head character, German, painted black eyes and painted teeth, cloth body, felt clothes, all original, slight crack to face.
....$150-$200

10" composition Patsy-type, marked "Germany," painted eyes, molded hair, wearing a gold-colored coat and hat; all original.
.... **$150-$225**

10" composition "ramp walker" black mammy that pushes a baby buggy, painted eyes and mouth, one arm has spring mechanism at elbow to allow it to hold onto buggy, wearing original polka-dot dress. Although the doll shows wear, it is still a desirable doll. .... **$200-$250**

Four 11" Dream World and National Costume Doll Co. dolls, 1940s, in various original costumes. .... **$75-$150 each, depending on appeal and costuming**

14" composition three-face Trudy by Three in One Doll Corp., faces changed by turning knob on top of head, paint peeling, redressed, marked "Sleepy Trudy, Weepy Trudy & Smiley Trudy." .... **$250-$300**

13" unmarked composition doll, made in Canada to resemble a Dionne Quint, brown tin eyes, jointed body, wearing original pink dress and bonnet; good condition. ....$200-$225

Two Peruvian composition figures, taller 15", wearing printed and painted embroidered clothing, all original. .... **$250-$300 each**

15" composition "Toni-type," blue-gray eyes, closed mouth, blonde wig, silver and blue taffeta dress and hat, redressed. .... **$150-$175**

16" composition head, molded hair, brown sleep eyes, closed mouth, resembles Patsy Joan doll, dress possibly original. .... **$100-$150**

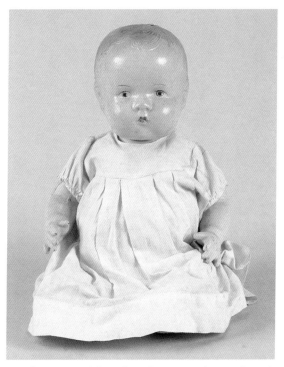

16 1/2" composition baby, maker unknown, painted eyes and mouth, original 1930s dress. ....,,... **$175-$225**

18" composition carnival doll, jointed at shoulders, painted eyes and mouth, appears repainted and redressed. ....**$50-$70**

If original ....**$150-$200**

18" composition child doll, unmarked, jointed, with blue tin sleep eyes, blonde wig, original rose-colored velveteen dress, "played with" condition.
.... $175-$225

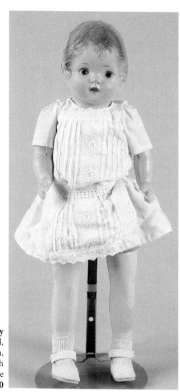

18" composition early child doll, unmarked, painted eyes and mouth, cotton body stuffed with excelsior, wearing a white dress. .... **$75-$100**

18" composition child doll, unmarked, jointed body, blue sleep eyes, closed painted mouth, blonde mohair wig, wearing a pink dress.
.... **$175-$200**

19" composition, unmarked, "Judy Garland-type," bent arms, gray sleep eyes, open mouth with teeth, wearing a white cotton dress with blue trim, "played with" condition. .... **$100-$150**

20" composition swivel head, marked "UNIS FRANCE 301" on back of head (UNIS is an acronym for the Union Nationale Inter-Syndicale, a mark found after 1915 on various French dolls produced by the Société Française de Fabrication des Bébés & Jouets), brown glass stationary eyes, open mouth with teeth, jointed composition body, wearing a rose-colored satin dress, brown boa, brown lace stockings, and leather shoes. .... $250-$350

21" composition head and limbs, marked "Made in Germany," blue sleep flirty eyes, open mouth and teeth, dressed in a blue knit suit and old leather shoes. .... $700-$900

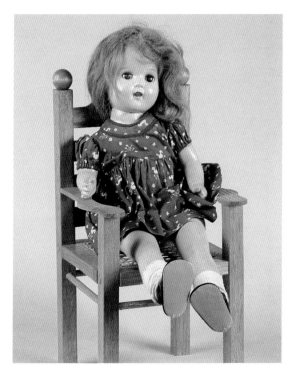

21" composition shoulder plate and limbs, unmarked, blue sleep eyes, open mouth with teeth, cloth body, wearing a blue print dress. . $150-$200

21" composition baby, unmarked, molded hair, brown sleep eyes, open mouth, cloth body, poor condition, redressed in a yellow dress, replaced shoes. ....$75-$100

21" composition, un-marked, jointed, brown sleep eyes, closed mouth, wearing bridesmaid dress. .... **$200-$250**

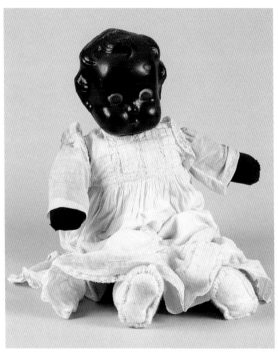

22" black composition, cloth body with composition hands, plastic-covered flirty eyes, molded hair, redressed in a white cotton dress, rare and desirable. .... $350-$500

23" Mama Baby, composition head and limbs, unmarked, brown tin sleep eyes, open mouth and teeth, wearing original white dress and sunbonnet; some crazing. .... **$250-$300**

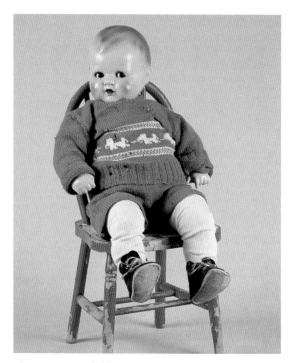

23" composition, marked "Germany 352W7," brown flirty sleep eyes, open mouth and tongue, molded hair, cloth body, wearing blue knit suit.
.... **$750-$1,000**

24" composition head, made in Italy, blue flirty eyes, closed mouth, jointed composition body (except for elbows and knees), appears in original good condition, wearing a brown taffeta dress and hat, only needs to be refreshed to bring her back to display condition. .... $600-$700

Metal-Head Dolls

The chief manufacturing center for metal-head dolls was in Germany at Nossen, Saxony. The familiar tin heads, dating from the turn of the 20th century to the 1930s, were cut and stamped from sheet metal, then welded together. These inexpensive heads were often sold separately, usually as replacements for the easily broken doll heads of bisque or china. This explains why metal heads are found on various body types. The painted or enameled surfaces are easily chipped and cracked.

13" METAL SHOULDER HEAD
13" metal shoulder head, unmarked, blue tin sleep eyes, composition hands, closed mouth, poor condition, wearing a cream-colored baby dress. ....$50-$60

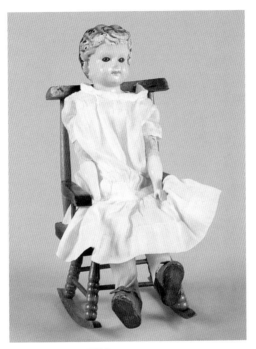

13" METAL SHOULDER HEAD
13" metal shoulder head, marked "Germany 55," blue glass eyes, closed mouth, cloth body, china hands, fair condition, wearing a white cotton dress and leather shoes. ....$75-$110

14" METAL SHOULDER HEAD
14" metal shoulder head, marked "Germany" on back shoulder plate, blue threaded glass eyes, open mouth with teeth, brown wig, china hands, kid body, appears in good, redressed condition, wearing a white cotton dress and black shoes. .... **$150-$200**

METAL SHOULDER HEAD MINERVA
16" metal shoulder head, marked "Minerva" on chest, painted blue eyes, closed mouth, composition hands, worn condition, wearing a maroon hooded cape with lace dress. .... **$100-$125**

METAL SHOULDER HEAD MINERVA

17" metal shoulder head, marked "Minerva" on chest, painted blue eyes, open mouth blonde hair, worn condition, wearing a black cape with fur collar.
.... **$100-$125**

19" METAL SHOULDER HEAD

19" metal shoulder head, unmarked, blue stationary glass eyes, open mouth, blonde wig, leather body, bisque hands, wearing a cotton dress, pink socks and shoes; near mint, seldom found in this condition. .... $275-$325

Papier-Mâché and Wax Dolls

Papier-mâché and wax dolls are combined here because the two materials are frequently paired on the same figure.

PAPIER-MÂCHÉ

Various manufacturers—mostly German—made doll heads using papier-mâché. A 19th century dictionary defined papier-mâché as "a tough plastic material made from paper pulp containing a mixture of sizing, paste, oil, resin, or other substances or from sheets of paper glued and pressed together." The wood and rag fibers in paper were responsible for much of early papier-mâché's strength.

Papier-mâché, carton paté (French), and holz-masse (German) are interchangeable terms for this paper-based material. Such dolls were individually handmade as early as the 16th century, but the development of the pressure-mold process in the early 1800s allowed papier-mâché dolls to be mass-produced.

WAX

Wax dolls were produced as early as the Middle Ages in Italy and other parts of Europe. There are three types: wax-over dolls, poured-wax dolls, and reinforced-wax dolls. The most frequently found problem with wax dolls is restoration. A network of minute age lines on an original surface is always more desirable than a newly re-waxed surface. If the surface is perfectly smooth with no cracks, dents, or scuff marks, chances are it has been re-waxed.

Occasionally someone will try to "fix" a wax doll by re-melting it (perhaps with hot spoons or a curling iron) or by having the head re-dipped. Attempts at restoration may be detected by looking for dirt embedded in the wax. A clear wax outer layer on a poured wax doll is another sign, since the original wax was tinted. When re-waxing a doll, clear wax is often used as a sealing coat.

Wax-Over Dolls

Wax-over dolls were made by various companies in England, France, and Germany during the 1800s and into the early 1900s. While dolls of many different materials were waxed over, papier-mâché or composition were the most frequently used.

An article published in the February 1875 edition of *St. Nicholas* magazine describes the process as follows: "...a frightful looking object she is, with color enough for a boiled lobster. When she has received her color and got dry...she proceeds to the next operator who is the waxer. In the kettle is boiling clear white beeswax, and into it Miss Dolly has been dipped, and is being held up to drain. If she had been intended for a cheap doll, she would have received but one dip, but being destined to belong to the aristocracy of the doll world, she received several dips, each one giving her a thin coat of wax, and toning down her flaming complexion into the delicate pink you see. The reason she was painted so red...is that she may have the proper tint when the wax is on. And now comes the next process, which is coloring her face. In this room is a long table with several workmen, each of whom does only one thing. The first one paints Miss Dolly's lips and sets her down on the other side of him. The next one takes her up and puts on her eyebrows. The third colors her cheeks. The fourth pencils her eyelashes, and so she goes down the table, growing prettier at every step..."

By the 1880s, paraffin or "ozocerite" (sometimes called ader wax, earth wax, mineral wax, or "ozokerite"), made from the residue of petroleum, was used instead of beeswax. The presence of beeswax can usually be detected by its distinct odor. Although not nearly as lifelike as the poured-wax or reinforced-wax dolls, the wax-over dolls have generally survived in better condition.

Poured-Wax Dolls

Poured-wax dolls are extremely lifelike, and by the mid-1800s, such dolls were being produced as toys, but with price tags that limited their purchase to a privileged few.

The time required to make a poured-wax doll was lengthy. First, a clay sculpture was crafted and a plaster of paris mold was made. This was accomplished by burying the clay head halfway in sand and then pouring plaster over the top. When the mold hardened, it was removed from the sand. The procedure was repeated for the other half of the head. The wax, originally beeswax and later paraffin, was placed in a cloth sack and boiled in water. It was then skimmed and placed in another sack. This purifying process was repeated at least four or five times. Purified with its high melting temperature, carnauba (a hard brittle high-melting wax obtained from the leaves of the carnauba palm) was then added to the paraffin for stability. The wax was then bleached by cutting it into strips and placing it on porcelain slabs in the sun. The wax had to be kept cool; therefore, the porcelain slabs floated on water in order to keep the wax from melting. This bleaching process took about a week. After bleaching, the wax was colored by boiling it with lead dyes or vermilion. The melted wax was then poured into heated molds. Molds had to be heated in order to prevent ridges from forming when the wax was initially poured. After a few seconds, the two mold halves were fastened tightly together, and rotated so that the melted wax could evenly coat over the mold's entire internal surface. The molds were removed when the wax hardened. While the wax was still warm, glass eyes were inserted and the eyelids molded. Next, the features were painted and hair inserted. Finally, the completed head was attached to a cloth body with wax limbs.

Most poured-wax dolls are unmarked; occasionally a doll was stamped or engraved with a signature. The method used for attaching the hair, the finely molded eyelids, tinted wax, and well-defined poured-wax arms and legs are all indications for collectors to note.

Reinforced-Wax Dolls

Reinforced-wax doll heads are generally accepted as having been made in Germany from about 1860 until 1890. They share many characteristics with poured-wax dolls. The method for making reinforced-wax heads begins with the poured-wax process. The head is then reinforced from within by means of a thin layer of plaster of paris or with strips of cloth soaked in a bonding agent, like composition. The intention of this reinforcement is to give the head added strength.

MAKERS OF PAPIER-MÂCHÉ AND WAX DOLLS

Ludwig Greiner, active mid-19th century

Records show Ludwig Greiner was listed as a toy maker in Philadelphia as early as 1840. In 1858, Greiner received the first known United States patent for a papier-mâché doll's head. The patent reads: "1 pound of pulped white paper, 1 pound of dry Spanish Whiting, 1 pound of rye flower [sic] and 1 ounce of glue reinforced with linen (strips of linen or silk lined the inside of the head adding strength), painted with oiled paint so that children may not pick off the paint." The heads were then given a layer of varnish, which has often served to protect the labels. A doll with the '58 patent date is known as "Early Greiner," whereas an 1872 extension date is known as a "Later Greiner."

Greiner papier-mâché heads have molded, wavy hair that gives the appearance of a high forehead and rather broad face, plus a snub nose and tight mouth.

GREINER PAPIER-MÂCHÉ

12" Greiner papier-mâché with '58 label. Black hairdo with exposed ears, blue eyes and on a cloth body with leather arms. Wearing only original underwear. Right arm has split to leather at elbow. Paint is all original and untouched, minor scuff to nose. .... $700-$800

GREINER PAPIER-MÂCHÉ
21" Greiner, deep shoulder head, black molded hair, brown painted eyes, cloth body, leather hands, wearing a tan cotton dress. ....**$1,000-$1,400**

OTHER PAPIER-MÂCHÉ
AND WAX DOLLS

PAPIER-MÂCHÉ MILLINER'S MODEL
9" German papier-mâché milliner's model with wardrobe, with curls descending onto the back of her neck. Several garments are included along with a box of miniature books. Overall condition is very good. Doll shows crazing and varnish loss to face.

Doll alone .... $350-$400
Doll with trunk and accessories... $700-$800

PAPIER-MÂCHÉ BABY
10" papier-mâché shoulder head baby, mechanical mouth (mechanism in body controls mouth, which opens when stomach is pressed), blue stationary glass eyes, cardboard body, cloth and composition hands and feet, wearing a white baby dress and bonnet, rare, nicely presented.... **$400-$450**

PAPIER-MÂCHÉ MILLINER'S MODEL
13 1/2" **German milliner's model** with long braids. All original, late 1830s. Dressed in a gauze outfit highlighted by red silk ribbon and lace. Exposed ears and long braids. Some scuffing to face, ... $750-$900

PAPIER-MÂCHÉ DOLLS

Two papier-mâché dolls, one with a 10" cloth body with wood limbs, replaced right arm; the second with an 11" cloth body with wood arms and legs. Nice condition. .... **$600-$800/pair**

PAPIER-MÂCHÉ FRENCH
10" French papier-mâché with painted eyes and pate with human hair attached. Wig slightly detached and original nail holes (to keep wig in place) are visible. Pink kid body (faded) and is not wearing original clothing, but has original underwear. Overall very fine original untouched condition. Small scuff to nose and some soiling to side of face. .... **$800-$1,000**

PAPIER-MÂCHÉ LADY
15" French papier-mâché lady with painted skullcap, applied human hair wig and a pink kid body (slight fading to body). Dressed in period clothing, lacking shoes. Condition is very fine with no apparent repainting to papier-mâché. ....$900-$1,200

PAPIER-MÂCHÉ MILLINER'S MODEL
16" German papier-mâché lady with rare hairdo, milliner's model. Doll has molded bun in back and braided tendrils. Silk sea-foam green high-waisted dress with gathered sleeves. Very good condition, although head has crazing to papier-mâché and black light reveals overpaint to breastplate.

.... $1,700-$2,000

PAPIER-MÂCHÉ MAN
18" German papier-mâché man. Short, curly black hair with brown painted eyes and is on a French kid body. Wearing a velvet overcoat with plaid vest and wool knickers. Head has lots of crackling and lifting of surface. ....**$500-$600**

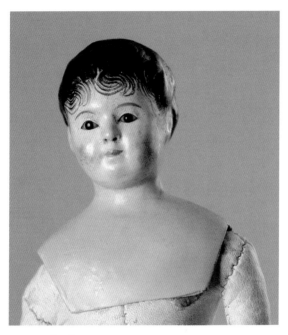

PAPIER-MÂCHÉ MAN
18" German glass-eyed papier-mâché man, with molded black hair and painted curls on forehead, also having pierced nostrils on a milliner-type body. Overall condition is good; there has been repair and touch-up to molded shoulder plate and head ....$1,700-$2,000

PAPIER-MÂCHÉ
23" papier-mâché shoulder head, blue stationary eyes, blonde wig, closed mouth, composition body and hands, leather boots, wearing a white and blue print dress with white apron, and a white lace bonnet with blue ribbon, appears in good condition. .... $400-$500

PAPIER-MÂCHÉ CHILD
15" beautiful early German papier-mâché child. On gusseted leather body with bisque lower arms. Blue paperweight eyes and blonde mohair wig. Dressed in antique clothes with early shoes and socks. Appears in very good condition. .... **$600-$750**

**PAPIER-MÂCHÉ
SHOULDER HEAD**
32" papier-mâché shoulder head, brown stationary glass eyes, brown wig, closed mouth, cloth body stuffed with excelsior, composition hands and lower legs, molded socks and shoes, wearing a cream-colored lace net dress, face appears badly worn, wig probably replaced; appropriately costumed, "as is" condition. .... $75-$100

PAPIER-MÂCHÉ SHOULDER HEAD

34" papier-mâché shoulder head, large brown stationary eyes, closed mouth, replaced brown wig, cloth body stuffed with excelsior, composition hands and feet, wearing a pink plaid dress with lace collar, appears in fair condition.

.... $200-$225

PAPIER-MÂCHÉ KÄTHE KRUSE-TYPE

Left, **14" papier-mâché swivel head** (Käthe Kruse-type), cloth-stuffed body, painted blue side-glancing eyes, closed mouth, wearing green felt dress and replaced black leather shoes; all original, "played with" condition.
.... **$100-$150**

Right, **13" papier-mâché** (Käthe Kruse-type), painted eyes, molded hair, cotton-stuffed joined body, wearing felt romper and shorts; all original.
....**$450-$500**

PAPIER-MÂCHÉ
SHOULDER HEAD
18" papier-mâché shoulder head, painted brown eyes, sparse blonde mohair wig, cotton-stuffed jointed body, wearing traditional German outfit of tan shorts, white shirt, red tie, costume damaged, face rubs and scuffed, missing shoes. .... **$50-$75**

WAX CHILD

13" German wax child with trunk and wardrobe. Inset blue glass eyes, dark blonde mohair wig, on a cloth body with squeaker in torso, and composition lower limbs. With additional costumes and accessories. Doll is encased in a leather trunk. Overall good condition. The trunk with additional costumes adds to the value of this doll..$1,000-$1,200

REINFORCED WAX SHOULDER HEAD

15" reinforced wax shoulder head, pierced ears, blonde wig, blue stationary eyes, composition arms and legs, painted shoes and socks, wearing a lavender dress. **$350-$400**

WAX-OVER PAPIER-MÂCHÉ BARTENSTEIN
15" two-face Bartenstein wax-over papier-mâché baby (Fritz Bartenstein, after 1880). Glass inset eyes, one face is smiling, the other is open mouthed and crying. Motchmann-style body with two pull-cords; one for crier, the other to revolve head. Wax is in fair condition, having lost original luster and coloring. .... $400-$500

WAX LADY
16" wax fashion lady. Shoulder-head wax with glass inset eyes, cloth body and wax limbs. Legs have molded shoes and arms have molded gloves in place. All original, wearing a light red polished cotton gown with lace trim and sandy blonde mohair wig. .... $900-$1,000

WAX-OVER HEAD SCHMITT BÉBÉ

17" Schmitt Bébé with wax head (Schmitt et Fils, Paris, 1863-1891). Wax-over head on a marked Schmitt body, stamped on derrière with Schmitt mark and also has large oval stamp on torso. Inset blue threaded paperweight eyes, wearing antique clothing, shoes, and original wig. Wax has slight roughness to nose. .... **$3,200-$3,6000**

WAX-OVER PAPIER-MACHÉ SCHMITT BÉBÉ

13" French wax-over papier-maché Schmitt Bébé (Schmitt et Fils, Paris, 1863 to 1891). Dressed in regional costume, on a fully jointed and marked Schmitt body with Paris shop label on torso, face has scuffing and has yellowed, body has chipping around toe area. A wax-over Schmitt is so rare that there is a degree of forgiveness for a less than perfect example; even in this worn condition the doll appears to have retained her original costume and shop label, ...**$1,200-$1,400**

WAX FRENCHMEN
Two 17" wax Frenchmen. Painted facial detailing, papier-mâché bodies, and applied wigs. Dressed in military garb. Some discoloring to the wax faces.
.... **$1,000-$1,200/pair**

WAX FRENCHMEN
Two 17" wax Frenchmen. Painted facial detailing, papier-mâché bodies, and applied wigs. Dressed in traditional garb. Some discoloring to the wax faces, and one has a silk shirt with heavy deterioration. .... **$1,000-$1,200/pair**

WAX ENGLISH LADY
18" English wax lady. Mohair wig, blue inset eyes with detailed eyebrows and painted upper and lower eyelashes. Lower arms and legs are wax. Wearing antique, probably original clothing, which shows some stress to the fabric. Some visible hairlines on forehead and side of head. .... **$700-$900**

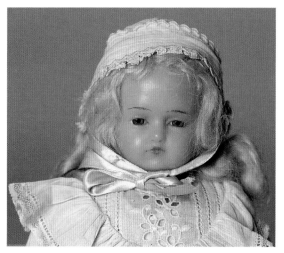

WAX ENGLISH BABY
18" English wax baby. Blue glass eyes and inset blonde hair on a cloth body with wax limbs, wearing an antique christening gown and matching bonnet. .... $350-$400

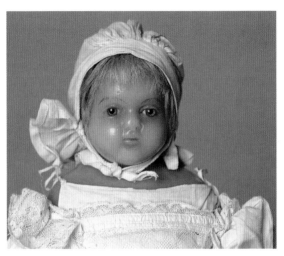

SIGNED WAX BABY
20" English wax baby signed "Lucy Peck." Blonde inset hair, blue glass eyes, and cloth body with wax lower limbs, wearing a cotton christening outfit and matching bonnet, some softening of features....................**$1,000-$1,400**

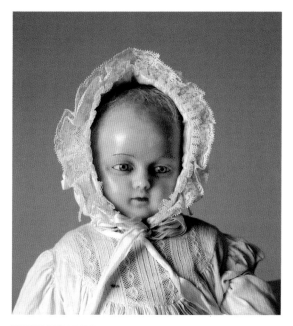

WAX ENGLISH BABY
20" English wax baby. Inset blonde hair (somewhat sparse), cheek coloring, on a cloth body with wax lower limbs, wearing an antique christening gown with matching bonnet. Overall very good condition, very appealing.
....$1,700-$2,000

WAX ENGLISH BABY
20" English wax baby with blue inset eyes, applied and painted hair, on a
cloth body with wax lower arms and legs, wearing an antique white cotton
christening gown and lace bonnet. Beautifully costumed, appealing. Pinkie
missing on right hand.
With finger damaged ....$1,500-$1,700
Perfect condition ....$1,700-$2,000

WAX ENGLISH LADY

20" English wax lady. Turned shoulder-head wax with brown inset eyes and costume with long train. Composition lower arms and lower legs with molded high heeled shoes. Body is cloth stuffed with excelsior. Some loss to painted highlights. .... **$600-$900**

WAX ENGLISH BABY
24" English wax baby. Blue glass sleep eyes, inset hair, and wax lower limbs, wearing antique white cotton dress and matching bonnet. Left leg has collapsed inward; in "as is" condition with loss to lip and face color and damaged leg. .... $500-$600

WAX SHOULDER HEAD

27" glass-eyed wax shoulder head doll with inset brown pupil-less eyes, brown curled wig and silk dress (extremely frail), on a cloth body with leather arms (probably early replacements). Has "dent" to wax below chin, paint loss to lip and face coloring, "as is" condition..........................$75-$125

WAX-OVER HALF DOLL
17" ladies half doll, 1920s, used to cover powder boxes, etc., turned wax-over head with arms joined to torso by wire, blonde mohair wig, wearing a skirt of beige painted net.. **$75-$100**

WAX-OVER SHOULDER HEAD
19" wax-over composition shoulder head, brown eyes, brown wig, closed mouth, cloth body, composition hands and lower legs, wearing a green velvet dress with knitted lace collar; appears to have been re-waxed, "as is" condition. ....$50-$60

Porcelain Dolls

BISQUE, CHINA, AND PARIAN

Bisque, china, and parian are all made of clay, feldspar, and flint. This mixture may be molded or poured, fired, painted, and fired again. Bisque is unglazed porcelain, usually with a flesh color and a matte finish. China is glazed porcelain (see China-Head Dolls). Parian is unglazed porcelain, but without a tint (see Parian Dolls).

Pink bisque is not painted, but rather tinted pink. Painted all-bisque dolls have paint applied as a thin wash over the entire body after firing.

In fine antique dolls, bisque may appear almost translucent, whether it is used only for doll heads or for the whole figure. Though there are exceptions, early antique dolls tend to have bisque that is pale. Before 1880, most bisque heads were of the shoulder-head type, with or without a swivel. The earliest bisque, china, and parian dolls were pressed into a mold by hand, while later examples were poured using clay slip.

Condition

An antique bisque doll head considered to be in excellent condition is one without cracks, hairlines, repairs, rubs, or "wig pulls."

A line or chip in an antique bisque head that can be seen with the naked eye is considered a crack. Chips often appear near the base of a bisque socket head or at the eye rim.

A fine imperfection that occurred during the initial firing of the bisque doll is referred to as a firing line. These are often filled with color that seeped in during the first firing. Firing lines are considered more stable than hairlines that develop later, and many collectors look upon them as minor imperfections when found on areas of an antique bisque head that are not obvious.

A fine crack that appears on an antique bisque head after initial manufacture is called a hairline, and these may be so fine that they cannot be seen with the naked eye. Hairlines may be spotted by using either a strong magnifying glass on the outside of the head or by placing the doll's open head (without pate and wig) under a bright light. They may appear as fine threads running through the bisque. A bisque doll head with a hairline is worth less than one without, and a hairline on the face lowers the value more than a hairline on the back of the head.

Antique bisque dolls should have smooth, clear bisque. As the name implies, "pepper marks" are black specks indicating there were impurities present when the head was manufactured. Absolutely perfect bisque heads are not common, so light speckling or pepper marks in inconspicuous places are considered minor.

Collectors use the term "rub" to describe places on antique bisque where the original color has worn off. Such an area may appear white. If the rubbing occurs in an inconspicuous area, it has little effect on the value of the doll.

Some antique dolls may be found with wigs glued to the top of the bisque head. When the wig is removed by pulling it off instead of using a product to dissolve the glue, some of the paint layer may be removed with the wig. This will leave areas of white exposed bisque, generally near the crown, called a "wig pull." Such areas are usually hidden when the wig is replaced. It has little effect on the value of the doll. (See price adjustment charts on pages 18-19.)

BISQUE DOLL HEADS

Henri Alexandre, 1888 to 1895

Located in Paris, Henri Alexandre was in existence for only a few years before being purchased by Tourrell Co., which merged with Jules Steiner in 1895. Alexandre designed the line of Phenix bébés, of which there were 30 models. Phenix bébés were manufactured for many years, eventually by Jules Steiner.

PHENIX BÉBÉ
19" Henri Alexandre Phenix Bébé (also spelled Phoenix Bébé). Even bisque, blue paperweight eyes and a fully jointed composition body. Marked on the rear of head "92." Wearing a replacement human hair wig and a French-style dress, with jacket and matching bonnet. White spot on tip of nose. Composition body is in very good original condition, with minor wear at joints. .... **$4,800-$5,300**

HENRI ALEXANDRE BÉBÉ

17" French Henri Alexandre Bébé. Marked on rear of head "H7A" with a "5" below the crown. Closed mouth with blue paperweight eyes, mauve eye shadowing. On a fully jointed composition French body. Wearing an antique cotton hounds-tooth dress with silk and lace trimmings, antique leather shoes, and a newer French human hair wig. Body shows signs of wear at joints and overall is somewhat soiled. ....$5,500-$6,000

Alt, Beck & Gottschalck, 1854 to 1930

Alt, Beck & Gottschalck was located in Nauendorf, near Ohrdruf, Thuringia, Germany, from 1854 until 1930. Along with the traditional bisque child and character babies, A.B.G., as it is commonly known, is credited by most doll historians with producing a series of beautifully detailed glazed and unglazed shoulder heads.

ALT, BECK & GOTTSCHALCK GERMAN BISQUE 18" German bisque A.B.G. turned shoulder head marked "8." Brown sleep eyes and open mouth with teeth. On a kid body with bisque lower arms and cloth lower legs. Redressed in a lady's costume and a newer wig and hat. Thumb on right hand is broken, and there is a small scuff to left brow. "As is" condition. .... **$500-$600**

ALT, BECK & GOTTSCHALCK BISQUE
36" bisque head, marked "Made in Germany ABG 1362 6 1/2," blue stationary eyes, open mouth with teeth, replaced papier-mâché and cardboard jointed body, wearing an elaborate cotton eyelet and lace dress, replaced wig, redressed, "as is" condition. ....**$1,400-$1,600**

Louis Amberg & Son, 1878 to 1930

Located in Cincinnati, Ohio, in 1878, and in New York from 1893 until 1930, Amberg imported and manufactured bisque and composition dolls. When Joshua Amberg joined his father in 1907, the firm became Louis Amberg & Son. In 1909, Amberg was listed as the artist/owner of "Lucky Bill," the first known American doll head to be copyrighted. In the late 1920s, Amberg advertised more than 600 style numbers (including some from French and German makers). Louis Amberg & Son was sold to E.I. Horsman in 1930.

AMBERG
BABY PEGGY
24" "Baby Peggy" By Louis Amberg. Closed-mouth character with brown sleep eyes on a "kidolene" body and bisque lower arms. Wearing a pink cotton dress, straw bonnet, antique brown leather shoes, and a replaced human hair wig. Body has some sawdust leakage. ....**$2,400-$2,800**

Bähr & Pröschild, 1871 to 1910

The dolls made at the Bähr & Pröschild porcelain factory in Ohrdruf, Germany, bear marks that help to date them. Prior to the late 1880s, dolls were marked with a mold number only. In 1888, "dep" (a claim to registration) was added. About 1895, the initials "B&P" were included. In 1900, a crossed-swords symbol made its appearance. In 1910, when Bruno Schmidt purchased the business, Bähr & Pröschild doll marks included a heart.

BÄHR & PRÖSCHILD CHARACTER BABY
11" bisque head character baby, marked "Bähr & Pröschild, 585 Germany," open/closed mouth, painted teeth, blue sleep eyes, jointed composition baby body, wearing a white romper with organdy and lace, replaced wig, good condition......... **$600-$750**

BÄHR & PRÖSCHILD CHARACTER BABY

12" bisque head character baby, marked "Bähr & Pröschild," open mouth, stationary blue eyes, composition baby body, wearing an aqua knit outfit, replaced wig, inappropriately dressed, body shows wear. .... **$450-$500**

BÄHR & PRÖSCHILD CHARACTER BABY

13" bisque head character baby, marked "585 Germany," open mouth with teeth and tongue, brown sleep eyes, composition baby body, wearing a long white cotton dress, appears in good condition. .... **$700-$850**

E. Barrois, 1844 to 1877

Located in Paris, E. Barrois was one of the earliest manufacturers of porcelain-head dolls in France. China heads have painted eyes and attached wigs. Most are shoulder heads, although a few socket heads on separate shoulder plates can be found. Lady bodies are made of kid or cloth. Hands are either kid with stitched fingers, or wooden upper arms with bisque hands. Sizes range from about 9" to 23" with a sizing code 3/0 to 7. Typical markings include "E (size number) B," "E (size number) Déposé B," and "EB."

BARROIS-TYPE POUPÉE

17" French bisque Poupée Barrois-type. Stationary shoulder head fashion with blue eyes on jointed wood body with bisque lower arms. Dressed in an antique two-piece walking suit and antique underwear. Original cork pate and blonde mohair wig. Eye chips on both lower eyelids. Body has original finish to wood. One missing pinkie on right hand. Costume in frail condition. .... **$3,500-$3,800**

BARROIS-TYPE FRENCH FASHION
17" Barrois-type French fashion. Pale bisque, blue threaded paperweight eyes on a kid body with composition lower arms (left thumb missing) and legs. Original wig, which is sparse, and original camel-colored dress with dark brown fringe. Some deterioration to outfit, lacking shoes. .... **$4,000-$4,800**

BARROIS-TYPE POUPÉE
18" French bisque Poupée Barrois-type. Shoulder head with cobalt blue eyes and fine facial detail. Kid-over-wood body with bisque lower arms, wearing a two-piece navy blue wool suit with antique blouse, underwear, and hat. Three fingers on the right hand are broken off and four fingers on the left. ....**$4,400-$4,900**

Belton-Type, after 1870

Although generally regarded as French, the beautiful Belton dolls with the distinguishing characteristic of the uncut pate section were probably manufactured by various firms in Germany in the last quarter of the 19th century. The top of the head may be concave, flat, or convex with one, two, or three holes. Common attributes also include a good quality wig; closed mouth; paperweight eyes with long painted lashes; and pierced ears. They range in size from about 9" to 24" tall.

BELTON-TYPE BISQUE HEAD
9" bisque head with flat base, Belton type, marked "3/0," two holes in head, blue glass stationary eyes, composition body, molded black shoes and socks, redressed. .... **$700-$900**

BELTON-TYPE CHILD
15" Belton-type 137 child. Pale bisque, dressed in an antique blue and black two-piece French-style outfit and matching bonnet (lacking shoes). On a straight-wrist, fully jointed body. Small eye chip, one on each upper eye rim. ....**$1,200-$1,500**

C. M. Bergmann, 1888 to 1931

C. M. Bergmann, located in Waltershausen, Germany, specialized in ball-jointed composition bodies with bisque heads. The heads came from several makers, including Alt, Beck & Gottshalck, Armand Marseilles, Simon & Halbig, and William Goebel. The dolls were distributed in the United States by Louis Wolf & Co., which registered some Bergmann trademarks, including "Baby Belle," "Cinderella Baby," and "Columbia."

BERGMANN BISQUE HEAD
24" bisque head, marked "287 CM Bergmann, BBI Germany," green stationary eyes, open mouth with teeth, composition body with stick legs, redressed, wearing green dress and hat, replaced wig. .... **$500-$600**

**BERGMANN
CHARACTER BOY**
**36" bisque head character
boy,** marked "CM Berg-
mann Waltershausen 1916
13," brown stationary eyes,
open mouth with teeth,
fully jointed body, wearing
green wool outfit, appealing, nicely costumed.
.....................$2,300-$2,500

BERGMANN SIMON & HALBIG
31" marked "CM Bergmann Simon & Halbig 14 1/2," blue sleep eyes, open mouth with teeth, pierced ears, blonde wig, fully jointed composition body, wearing a beige lace dress and straw bonnet. ....**$1,200-$1,400**

Bru Jne & Cie, 1866 to 1899

Founded by Leon Casimir Bru, the firm that was located in Paris and Montreuil-sous-Bois, France, is often simply called Bru. Bru dolls fall into three categories: bébé on a kid body, Bru doll on a wood-and-composition body, and fashion ladies, or poupee de modes.

The Societé Française de Fabrication de Bébés & Jouets, founded in 1899, continued to make Bru dolls and bébés. The S.F.B.J. later resurrected the Bru trademark, in 1938 and 1953.

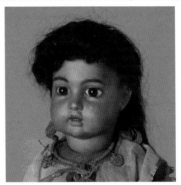

CIRCLE DOT BRU
13" Brown Circle Dot Bru. Marked with a dot within a circle and number "3" on head, "BRU JNE" on shoulder plate and stamped "BÉBÉ BRU #3" on leather torso. Amber eyes with even brown bisque, bisque arms and chevrot-style body and wearing antique (possibly original) ethnic clothing; 1" hairline from right ear to crown. Minor cheek scuffs and a pin flake to lower right eye rim.
"As is" condition .... $10,000-$12,000
Perfect condition $30,000

BRU FASHION
13 1/2" all original Bru fashion. Swivel-neck (marked "C" on head) on a gusseted kid body with blue paperweight eyes and fine pale bisque. Dressed in a sea-foam green silk gown with pleated train; white feather boa, outfit adorned with lace and flowers. Original wig and brown leather boots. Outfit frail with slight fraying on arms. ....$3,800-$4,200

NURSING BRU BÉBÉ

15" bisque nursing Bru Bébé Teteur. Original blonde mohair wig, cork pate, and original mechanism in head is still intact. Lace and gauze baby costume with pink silk ribbons is original. Layers of undergarments and original buttoned diaper on a fully jointed composition French body. Body retains original finish with normal wear. Earring loop is chipped on left ear. Exceptional condition.. $10,000-$12,000

NURSING BRU
17" French bisque nursing Bru. Labeled Bru body with wood lower legs and replaced bisque arms. Large blue paperweight eyes and blonde mohair wig with cork pate. Wearing antique white baby gown with bottle attached. Bisque has some light dusting and inherent mold line under chin and a small scuff to right brow. Paperweight eyes are old replacement. Leather body in good condition. Lower legs are repainted. "As is" condition. .**$3,500-$4,000**

BRU JNE BÉBÉ
15" Bru Jne #4 Bébé.
Molded tongue with deep mottling, chevrot body and blue paperweight eyes. Blonde mohair wig and replaced French-style clothing. Restoration to crack running from top of head between left eye and ear, under chin and continuing behind the right ear to the top of head. Paint spray has been removed, exposing a small white line (1/4" wide) starting at lower ear and continuing under chin; this is not visible when wig is in place. Extra kid has been glued on at elbow joints. Leather body overall in good condition, wood lower legs have been repainted. Redressed, replaced shoes. "As is" condition
...................$5,000-$6,000
Perfect condition
.... $23,000-$27,000

Bru Poupée
15" French bisque Bru Poupée. Signed on shoulder plate. Swivel neck and stationary blue eyes, on a gusseted leather body. Dressed as an older child in a blue mariner's costume with detailed red stockings and red pocketbook with comb. Original human hair wig and antique ivory leather shoes. Light speckling across brows. Very appealing. ....$4,500-$5,300

BRU POUPÉE
15" French bisque Bru Poupée. Marked on shoulder plate. Blue glass eyes, wearing a two-piece heavy cotton antique walking suit and antique leather high-button boots. On a rare fully articulated straight-wrist wooden body, with human hair wig. Light speckling on chin and forehead, body finish has a lot of wear, especially to legs. ....$7,500-$8,000

BRU ORIENTAL FASHION
15" Oriental fashion attributed to Bru. Original human hair wig, on a fully jointed wood fashion body. Costumed in silk embroidered kimono and straw hat with wax flowers, antique underwear, and brown leather boots. Rare and appears in perfect original condition. .... **$21,000-$23,000**

BRU JNE BÉBÉ

19" French bisque Bru Jne Bébé. Molded brows and brown paperweight eyes. Peaches and cream bisque and well-defined tongue. Wearing original costume including marked Bru shoes, original chemise, and original blonde mohair wig. On Chevrot body with wood lower legs and bisque arms. Fine dusting to bisque on chin. Some moth damage to costume. Original, fine condition..**$32,000-$37,000**

BRU JNE BOY
21 1/2" French bisque open mouth Bru Jne. R 9 boy. Brown sleep eyes; open mouth with molded teeth, brown mohair wig, dressed in a replaced brown velvet suit. Lower right lashes have a repaired chip affecting five lashes. Small scuff to lip paint. On appropriate jointed composition body.
.... $2,000-$2,400

BRU JNE R BÉBÉ
23" Bru Jne R Bébé. Blue paperweight eyes, even complexion bisque, on a fully jointed composition and wood Bru body (unmarked). Wearing antique French leather shoes, original underwear and appropriate French-style silk dress with matching hat. Flaking on lower arms and derriere, minor cheek scuff to lower left cheek, scuff on upper lip and minute eye flake to upper lid of left eye. ....$6,000-$7,500

Cuno & Otto Dressel, 1873 to 1942

Though generations of the Dressel family operated a toy business in Germany, starting in the 18th century, the firm headed by Cuno and Otto Dressel was established in 1873. The company purchased bisque doll heads from several makers, including Ernst Heubach, Gebrüder Heubach, Armand Marseille, and Simon & Halbig.

CUNO & OTTO DRESSEL FLAPPER 14" C.O.D. 1469 flapper/ character lady. Dressed in appropriate lace style attire. Brown mohair wig with blue glass sleep eyes. Shoes are replacements but clothing probably original. Minor wear to body, some paint loss to ball joints. Appealing. **$3,700-$4,200**

CUNO & OTTO DRESSEL GERMAN MAN
14" German character man. Marked on rear of head "M 1," probably manufactured by Cuno & Otto Dressel. Brown set eyes with open mouth on a jointed composition body. Wearing an original man's wool outfit with matching blue cap and blonde mohair wig. Straight-wrist composition body in very fine original condition. Lacking shoes. Minor moth damage to pants. ....$2,000-$2,400

GERMAN CUNO & OTTO DRESSEL
23" German bisque C.O.D. marked "1349." Dressed in 1920s lady fashion, blue sleep eyes, on a fully jointed German composition body. All fingers on left hand are missing, extensive wear to lower torso.

With body damage ....$800-$1,000
Perfect condition ....$1,200-$1,300

Eden Bébé, 1873 to 1920s

The doll with this trade name was made by the Fleischmann and Bloedel Doll Factory in Fürth, Bavaria, and Paris. The company became a charter member of the Societé Française de Fabrication de Bébés & Jouets in 1899.

EDEN BÉBÉ
26" French Eden Bébé. Open mouth, brown paperweight eyes. On a fully jointed French composition body (right hand re-painted and chipping) and wearing some antique underwear; 2" hairline on center of forehead (covered by wig) and small mold flaw in corner of right eye. "As is" condition. **$900-$1,100**

French Bisque Fashion-Type

Known as poupée de modes or just poupées, these adult-bodied and fashionably dressed dolls were manufactured primarily between 1860 and 1930 in France, Germany and, to a lesser degree, Austria. Bisque heads are found on bodies of cloth, kid, or wood.

Kid Body Poupée de Mode: pale, fine bisque swivel head; kid-lined bisque shoulder plate; fine gusseted kid body; bisque or kid arms with stitched fingers; good wig; exquisitely painted or paperweight eyes, finely lined in black; painted lashes; feathered brows; pierced ears; closed mouth; appropriately dressed; typically marked with size number only or unmarked.

Wooden Body Poupée de Mode: pale, fine bisque swivel head; kid-lined bisque shoulder plate; attached with kid to fully articulated wooden body; wooden peg joints; good wig; paperweight eyes, finely lined in black; painted, long lashes; softly feathered brows; pierced ears; small, closed mouth; appropriately dressed; typically marked with size number only or unmarked.

FASHION
13" painted-eye fashion.
Bisque shoulder-head with painted blue eyes, replaced cloth body with leather arms, and newer wig. "As is" condition. **$900-$1,000**

FASHION WITH TRUNK
16" unmarked French fashion with trunk. Gusseted kid body with swivel neck and all original from wig to shoes. Trunk/wardrobe includes extra costumes, hats, a parasol, and accessories. Clothing and kid body show some wear. This very desirable collection appears in excellent condition.
.... **$7,500-$9,000/set**

FASHION

16" shoulder head fashion. Pale bisque with blue eyes on a straight kid body with bisque arms (tip of right forefinger missing). Wearing an antique brown dress with black and gold ribbon trim and French leather shoes. Wig is a human hair replacement. Firing crack on shoulder plate under dress line.

.... $2,500-$3,000

FASHION MAN
21" French fashion man. Stiff neck, all original with cobalt blue eyes, fine bisque, and sandy blonde mohair wig on a gusseted kid body. Dressed in a black tuxedo with vest and shirt and a beaver skin top hat with a London label inside. Lacking shoes. Brown pin spots on left eyelid. ..**$3,200-$3,700**

Fulper Pottery Co., 1918 to 1921 (doll production only)

Originally founded in 1815 at Flemington, New Jersey, and known for its art pottery, Fulper produced bisque dolls and doll heads for less than five years.

FULPER BISQUE HEAD
20" bisque head, marked "Fulper Made in USA," open mouth with teeth, brown stationary eyes, fully jointed body, inappropriately redressed in a pink dress with white lace.
.... $400-$450

Francois Gaultier, 1860 to 1916

Located on the outskirts of Paris, Gaultier produced bisque doll heads for several firms, including Gesland, Jullien, Rabery & Delphieu, Simonne, and Thuiller. It later became part of the Societé Française de Fabrication de Bébés & Jouets.

GAULTIER FASHION DOLLS

Left, **11" bisque shoulder head fashion doll,** marked "F.G.," paperweight eyes, closed mouth pierced ears, leather hands, original wig, cloth body, redressed in purple and pink... **$1,500-$1,800.**

Right, **11" bisque shoulder head fashion doll,** marked "F.G.," paperweight eyes, closed mouth pierced ears, leather hands, original wig, cloth body, wearing original light green dress repaired with flowered print. .... **$1,500-$1,800**

GAULTIER BLACK POUPÉE
12" black French F.G. Poupée. Dark brown bisque and brown leather kid body. Black wig, wearing a costume made of antique fabrics and striped silk and red cotton with red matching hat. Normal wear to body. Minute scuff to tip of nose and lower lip. ....$2,000-$2,400

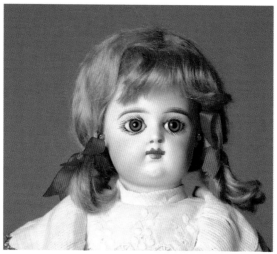

GAULTIER BÉBÉ

16" F.G. Bébé. Rear of head is marked with "F.G." in scroll. Blue paperweight eyes, pale bisque, on a five-piece, jointed wrist composition body. Wearing an antique white cotton dress and blonde mohair wig. Tiny flake to lower left eye rim. "As is" condition with later five-piece body and rather heavily applied facial features. ....**$2,400-$2,900**

GAULTIER FASHION
17" F.G. French fashion.
Blue paperweight eyes,
on a Gesland body with
bisque hands and lower
legs. Original condition
with a gauze and lace-
trimmed dress highlighted
with silk aqua ribbons.
Original blonde French
mohair wig and straw hat.
Beautiful, desirable doll in
excellent display condition
with a rare Gesland body.
.....................$6,500-$7,000

GAULTIER POUPÉE
18" French bisque F.G. Poupée. Jointed wood fashion body with antique two-piece sage green silk dress with matching hat and red corset, antique underwear, and black leather shoes. Wig is replaced sheepskin. Early repaint to body. "As is" condition. ....$4,500-$5,000

GAULTIER POUPÉE
20" French bisque F.G. Poupée. Blue spiral paperweight eyes, fine bisque. On a stockinette Gesland body with bisque limbs. Wearing an antique black walking suit with matching hat and original human hair wig with long woven braids in the back and original earrings. Minor pepper spots on cheek. Costume has some splits and wear to the skirt. Beautiful early, fine poupée with elaborate wig and rare Gesland body..................**$7,500-$8,200**

GAULTIER GESLAND BÉBÉ
21" F.G. Gesland Bébé. Marked body and rear of head "F.G." in scroll and size number "8." Bulbous light blue paperweight eyes, even bisque and pale lips with a hint of a tongue. Wearing a newer French-type outfit with coordinating hat and jacket. Composition lower arms, legs, and shoulder plate have had paint restoration and repair. Appropriately redressed; repainted body detracts from this otherwise lovely doll.
.... **$4,000-$4,500**

GAULTIER POUPÉE
24" French bisque F.G. Poupée. On gusseted French leather body. Redressed in gold and blue walking suit and wearing original blonde mohair wig. Restored on face, on both lower eyes, beneath the nose and across the upper lip. Body has minor repairs. "As is" condition ....**$1,000-$1,200**

GAULTIER POUPÉE
25" French bisque F.G. Poupée. Painted detail and pale gray eyes. Original blonde mohair wig, on a gusseted French body wearing an elaborate replaced gown and white leather boots. Minor scuff to chin. Body has some small patching to gussets and fingers. .... $4,000-$4,500

GAULTIER FASHION

29" F.G. fashion. Blue threaded paperweight eyes and fine bisque. On a gusseted kid body and wearing a floral print silk gown (minor deterioration) and antique leather shoes. Curly human hair wig with matching straw and fabric bonnet and comes with a black parasol. Repair to forehead. The location of the restoration of this doll is somewhat tolerable. "As is" condition. .... **$2,500-$2,700**

Gesland, 1860

Gesland dolls have outstanding body features of a steel frame wrapped with kapok or cotton, several with stockinette or lambskin, giving a natural shape. The realistically poseable bodies were marked "Bebe Gesland Paris."

GAULTIER GESLAND BÉBÉ
30" F.G. Gesland Bébé. Marked body, and on rear of head, "F.G." in scroll and size number "11." Hazel eyes, pale bisque, a newer pale blue frock with tatted lace, a long light brown human hair wig and closed mouth with molded tongue. Composition body parts have been repainted. Original spring in head connecting to shoulder plate. ....$5,900-$6,500

Goebel, founded 1876

Established in Bavaria by Franz D. Goebel, son William became sole owner of the porcelain factory in 1893, changing the name to William Goebel. Early Goebel bisque objects were marked with a triangle and a quarter moon. After 1900, a crown above a conjoined "W&G" was introduced.

GOEBEL CHARACTER BABY
14" bisque shoulder head character baby, marked with a crown and conjoined "WG" and "B5-3 Germany, Bavaria Goebel," brown sleep eyes, open mouth, composition baby body, wearing a white cotton dress.
..............$550-$600

A. Halopeau (H Mold), late 19th century

"H mold" dolls are attributed to Aristide Marcellin Halopeau of Paris. Halopeau was listed as a doll maker in the Paris annual register from 1881 until 1889.

HALOPEAU BÉBÉ
18" Halopeau Bébé. Threaded blue paper-weight eyes with sandy blonde mohair wig. Wearing an antique sea-foam green dress with matching hat, leather boots, and gloves. On a jointed composition Jumeau body. Slight nose rub. Beautifully presented doll. **$68,000-$75,000**

HALOPEAU BÉBÉ

24" Halopeau Bébé. Marked on rear of head "5 H," on a jointed, straight-wrist composition body. Threaded blue paperweight eyes, wearing an antique white cotton dress. Bisque restoration appears to be from top of eyelids up into the forehead and extending over to both ears. "As is" condition..**$3,000-$3,500**

Heinrich Handwerck, 1876 to 1930

Founded in Gotha, Thüringia, Germany, by Heinrich Handwerck Sr. and his wife, Minna, the company designed the bisque heads that were produced by Simon & Halbig. After Heinrich's death in 1902, the firm was purchased by Kämmer & Reinhardt of nearby Waltershausen.

HEINRICH HANDWERCK GIRL 19" girl by Handwerck, marked "Heinrich Handwerck–Simon Halbig–Germany," open mouth with teeth, brown stationary eyes, reddish hair, jointed composition body (appears new), wearing an old dress of stained apricot silk and black lace. "As is" condition with replaced body. .... **$450-$500**

HEINRICH HANDWERCK BODY

25" bisque head, marked "Made in Germany, 12 171," body marked "Heinrich Handwerck Germany," sleep eyes, blonde wig, open mouth with teeth, composition body, wearing a blue silk dress, white stockings, black shoes. This is a Kestner head on a marked Handwerck body. With replaced dress, socks, and shoes. "As is" condition. .... **$400-$500**

HEINRICH HANDWERCK BISQUE HEAD
28" bisque head, marked "Heinrich Handwerck, Simon & Halbig, 6 Germany," brown sleep eyes, open mouth with teeth, jointed composition body, wearing a pink dress with lace. Display condition.........**$1,600-$1,800**

Max Handwerck, founded 1899

Located in Walters-hausen, Thüringia, Germany, Max Handwerck designed and modeled the facial molds, many of which were produced as bisque doll heads by William Goebel.

MAX HANDWERCK BISQUE HEAD

25" bisque head, marked "Germany Max Handwerck," open mouth with teeth, fine brown wig, green threaded stationary eyes, fully jointed composition body, wearing a pink dress with heavy lace and a flowered headpiece. "As is" condition, eyes replaced.
.... $400-$450

Ernst Heubach, founded 1887

This manufacturer of bisque dolls was located in Köppelsdorf, Germany. In 1919, Heubach and Armand Marseilles merged, but later split in 1932. Dolls marked "Heubach Koppelsdorf" were produced between 1919 and 1932. Other marks include a horseshoe, the initials "E.H," in addition to various mold numbers.

ERNST HEUBACH BISQUE HEAD
9" bisque head, marked "Heubach Koppelsdorf, 320-9110 Germany," blue sleep eyes, open mouth with teeth, composition baby body, brown wig, wearing a white cotton and lace dress. .... **$275-$325**

ERNST HEUBACH TODDLER
18" bisque head character toddler, marked "Heubach Köppelsdorf, 320 Germany," brown stationary eyes, open mouth with teeth, composition five-piece toddler body, wearing a light pink dress and bonnet. .... **$800-$900**

ERNST HEUBACH SHOULDER HEAD
21 1/2" bisque shoulder head, marked "Heubach Köppelsdorf," blue stationary eyes, open mouth with teeth, kid body, wearing a cream-colored silk pleated dress with pink ribbon. .... **$300-$350**

ERNST HEUBACH BISQUE HEAD
26" bisque head, marked "Koppelsdorf Thuring," sleep eyes, jointed body, redressed for historical display. .... **$500-$550**

**ERNST HEUBACH
BISQUE HEAD**
27" bisque head, marked
"Heubach Koppelsdorf
250-6 1/2 Germany," open
mouth with teeth, blue
stationary eyes, replaced
wig, jointed composition
body, wearing a white
dress. .... **$500-$550**

Gebrüder Heubach, founded 1840

Heubach is not known to have made doll heads until about 1910, though the Heubach family bought an established porcelain factory in Lichte, Thüringia, Germany, in 1840. In addition to mold numbers, artist or sculptor initials may be included in the markings.

GEBRÜDER HEUBACH DOLL WITH TRUNK
7" Heubach character doll with trunk. Closed mouth, with blue glass eyes, jointed German composition body with bent arms and straight wrists, wearing gauze print dress and brown mohair wig in braids. Accompanied by trunk mounted with wardrobe and accessories. Minor wear at joints and small repair to neck socket. Doll appears in appropriate costume; trunk and accessories appear to be newer additions, ...$800-$1,000

GEBRÜDER HEUBACH ALL BISQUE
8" all bisque, marked "Heubach 95583," intaglio eyes; painted hair, socks and shoes; pink crocheted dress. .... **$850-$900**

GEBRÜDER HEUBACH LAUGHING TWINS
8 1/2" dome-head bisque laughing twins, marked "3/0 HEUBACH, Germany," all bisque jointed bodies, intaglio eyes, both wearing cotton suits. .... **$1,000-$1,200 each**

GEBRÜDER HEUBACH BISQUE DOME HEAD 11 1/2" bisque dome head, marked "0 Germany Gebrüder Heubach," blue intaglio eyes, closed mouth, (professional repair to head), wearing a blue wool suit and cap. "As is" condition, hands appear in poor condition. ....$100-$150

GEBRÜDER HEUBACH CHARACTER
14" Gebrüder Heubach 6969 character. Original provincial outfit (lacking shoes) with blue glass sleep eyes and fine bisque. Composition neck socket on body has been repaired. .... **$3,000-$3,200**

GEBRÜDER HEUBACH LAUGHING CHARACTER
15" Heubach 5636 laughing character. Blue glass sleep eyes, fine bisque and
open mouth with two molded teeth. On a German ball-jointed composition
body with a brown mohair wig and antique clothing. Slight scuff underneath
chin. ....**$3,200-$3,500**

GEBRÜDER HEUBACH CHARACTER GIRL
16" Heubach 7407 character girl. Brown sleep eyes, on ball-jointed composition body. Eye chip on lower left rim and hairline on rear of head going into a "Y." Doll is loosely strung and has replaced human hair wig. "As is" condition. .... $600-$650

GEBRÜDER HEUBACH CHARACTER CHILD
17" German bisque Heubach character child marked 8192. Antique blue gingham dress, original underwear, replaced newer shoes, and a blue straw hat. Wig is a good human hair replacement, with fully jointed composition body. Normal wear to finish. Very appealing............................**$1,100-$1,300**

GEBRÜDER HEUBACH SMILING LADY
18" Gebrüder Heubach smiling lady 7925. All original turned shoulder head with original outfit (frail). Composition lower arms and legs (molded socks and shoes) on a cloth body. Unusual size. Fine condition.
.... **$4,500-$5,000**

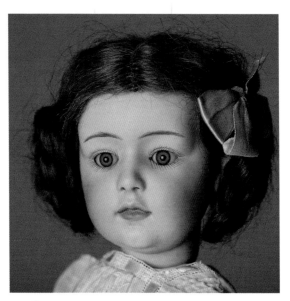

GEBRÜDER HEUBACH POUTY CHARACTER
20" Heubach 7374 pouty character. Blue glass sleep eyes, on a German ball-jointed composition body (finish on lower legs not consistent with remainder of body). Wearing an antique white dress highlighted with pink ribbons, a sandy brown human hair wig with braids over the ears, and antique leather shoes. Fine condition..$5,000-$5,500

Huret, second half of the 19th century

Based in Paris, Maison Huret was known for its gusseted kid and articulated wooden bodies. In 1861, it patented a socket swivel neck. Huret fashion dolls may also have china or tinted porcelain heads.

HURET CHILD
18" Huret child. On a fully articulated wood body. Light blue threaded paperweight eyes and closed mouth. Wearing an antique blue gingham dress with silk ivory blouse, curly blonde lamb's wool wig, antique watch and chain. Body has been stripped of paint and several fingers have been replaced.
.... $35,000-$40,000

HURET FASHION
18" marked, painted-eye
Huret fashion. Swivel
neck, painted cornflower
eyes. Leather torso has the
"Huret" stamp and address
of the firm. Wearing
antique costume with black
silk slippers (heels marked
"T" on the sole). With purchase provenance. Gutta
percha arms and jointed
lower legs have had repair
and repainting. Mohair
wig is a later replacement.
Very rare doll.
.... **$25,000-$28,000**

Jumeau, founded early 1840s

Pierre Francois Jumeau began manufacturing dolls in Paris and Montreuil-sous-Bois, France, in about 1842, in a partnership called Belton & Jumeau.

There are several Jumeau doll head markings. The most commonly found mark is the "Tete Jumeau" stamp and a red artist check mark. Earlier Jumeaus can be found marked "E.J." with a size number. The rare, long-faced Jumeau, as well as other portrait Jumeaus, are marked with a size number only.

JUMEAU DEP BÉBÉ
10" all original Jumeau DEP Bébé with trunk, German-made for French market. Impressed "DEP" and rubber-stamped "Jumeau" on rear of head. On a fully jointed French-style composition body, wearing antique lace dress, blue leather shoes, and white fleece coat and hat. Cork pate, original mohair wig, and brown glass sleep eyes. Included assorted outfits. Overall condition is very fine, some repair and touch-up to lower legs. Nice presentation.. ..,,....................$2,000-$2,400/set

JUMEAU PORTRAIT
11" second series portrait
Jumeau. Brown paper-weight eyes on a straight-wrist, eight-ball-jointed Jumeau body, marked with a "3" on rear of head. Brown French mohair wig, antique white dress, and French shoes. Minor wear to joints, wig is somewhat sparse. .... **$7,000-$7,500**

TETE JUMEAU
12" Tete Jumeau #3. Blue paperweight eyes, on a fully jointed and marked composition Jumeau body. Replacement (but old) maroon satin dress and antique undergarments. Minor wear at joints. Some paint and composition loss to right forearm. Wig is a newer replacement, lacking shoes.
....$4,200-$4,700

JUMEAU PORTRAIT
15" first series Jumeau portrait. Marked with "2/0," amber paperweight eyes with mauve eye shadowing, pale bisque on eight-ball-jointed body marked Jumeau. Wearing antique white low-waisted gauze dress and matching hat. Original cap to skin wig (lacking hair, but is now wearing sandy brown mohair wig). Jumeau shoes are marked "Jumeau Bébé Depose #6." Shoes are replaced Jumeau shoes. Doll loosely strung, original cap to skin wig has not been removed from head.
.... **$20,000-$22,000**

TETE JUMEAU
17" Tete Jumeau #7
with original box in pristine condition. Pale bisque and brown paperweight eyes on a fully jointed and marked composition Jumeau body. Original print dress with hat, cork pate, spring in head, original marked Jumeau shoes, and blonde mohair wig.
.... **$10,000-$12,000**

JUMEAU DÉPOSÉ E9J
19" Déposé E9J doll. Blue paperweight eyes and fine bisque on a straight-wrist, eight-ball-jointed Jumeau (unmarked) body. Wearing antique shoes, a pale green dress, large bow on the back and a pale green bonnet. Original spring in head. Minor wear and paint loss at body joints. .....**$8,700-$9,200**

DÉPOSÉ JUMEAU
19" incised Déposé Jumeau #8. Amber paperweight eyes on a straight-wrist fully jointed and marked Jumeau body. Extensive restoration to head, but still retains original spring connecting head to torso. Wearing newer style clothes and wig. Restoration primarily on forehead and bridge of nose. "As is" condition. .... **$900-$1,200**

TETE JUMEAU
22" Tete Jumeau #10. Bisque featuring amber eyes on a Jumeau ball-jointed composition body. Wearing a silk taffeta print dress and an older human hair wig with coiled braids covering each ear. Wear to joints. Good condition...$5,200-$5,700

JUMEAU BÉBÉ
22" French Jumeau Bébé marked "R.9.R." Closed-mouth with blue paperweight eyes and uniform bisque on an eight-ball-jointed Jumeau composition body. Wearing a newer dark blue French-style dress with a curly human hair wig and marked antique French leather shoes (frail condition). Body has been repainted, otherwise overall condition is very fine. ....$5,500-$6,000

LONG FACE JUMEAU
25" "long face" Jumeau.
Called a "Triste" Jumeau.
Marked on rear of head
with number "11" and is
on an eight-ball-jointed
marked Jumeau body,
also with Paris store label,
"JEUX & JOUETS." Pale
bisque with light mauve
shadowing, blue paper-
weight eyes, and sandy
blonde mohair wig.
Marked size "11" French
leather shoes (frail con-
dition) and wearing an
aqua checked wool frock
with feather stitching
and matching aqua hat.
Original spring in head,
but is loosely strung, and
has normal minor wear
to body joints. Very good
condition.
.... **$32,000-$35,000**

K&K Toy Co., founded 1915

The New York firm of K&K Toy Co. imported bisque heads from Germany and supplied cloth and composition bodies to other companies, including George Borgfeldt. Bodies were often marked "bisquette" or "fiberoid." Bisque K&K doll heads are found on cloth bodies with composition limbs or kid bodies with bisque arms.

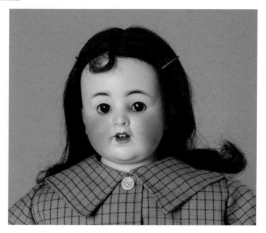

K&K TODDLER
23" K&K 60 bisque toddler. Shoulder-head toddler, on a "mama" type body. Brown sleep eyes, long dark human hair wig, original underwear, shoes and socks, and is wearing a plaid overcoat. Body appears to have original finish with very little wear. .... **$800-$900**

Kämmer & Reinhardt, founded 1886

Ernst Kämmer and Franz Reinhardt started their firm in Waltershausen, Thüringia, Germany, designing but not manufacturing doll heads. Simon & Halbig made most of the bisque heads and became part of Kämmer & Reinhardt by 1920.

The "W" found on the forehead of some Kämmer & Reinhardt dolls may refer to the Waltershausen region. Some numbers (starting with 15) found low on the doll's neck indicate sizes in centimeters, not mold numbers.

Kämmer & Reinhardt introduced its K(star)R character dolls on bent-limb baby bodies at the 1909 Munich Exhibit.

KÄMMER & REINHARDT WITH TRUNK
9" K(star)R/Simon & Halbig 21 with trunk. Open-mouth doll with blue sleep eyes, brown mohair wig (appears replaced), on a jointed German composition body with straight wrists. Redressed with newly created red dome-top trunk with several outfits. Some discoloration to lower arms, some wear at joints. ..... **$900-$1,100/set**

KÄMMER & REINHARDT GRETCHEN

12" K(star)R 114 "Gretchen." Pale blue eyes, on a pink fully jointed composition body. Dressed in a white cotton frock and blonde mohair wig with braids. Composition body has crazing to lower legs and some paint touch up throughout. Bisque has peppering, most noticeable on left cheek. Small white pinprick, also on left cheek. ....$2,800-$3,100

KÄMMER & REINHARDT KARL
12" German bisque K(star)R 107 character doll known as "Karl." Painted eyes, original mohair wig, wearing a newer brown velvet costume and antique oilcloth shoes. Fully jointed pink body has splits and crazing to legs. Rare.
.... $17,000-$20,000

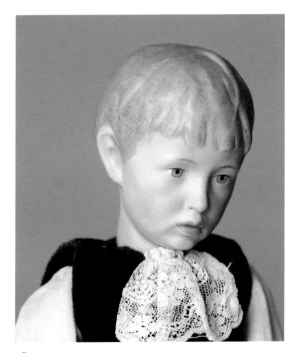

KÄMMER & REINHARDT WALTER
12" German bisque K(star)R 102, Walter, with molded hair. Wearing newer velvet costume. Small chip in neck socket. Light dusting to bisque. Fully jointed composition body in good condition. Rare. .... **$23,000-$25,000**

KÄMMER & REINHARDT MAX

16" K(star)R bisque character 123 known as "Max." Dressed in older clothes. Brown human hair wig and French body. Also included, one book featuring Max and Moritz characters. Two hairlines to back of head. French body has wear on hands and is a replacement. "As is" condition.

.... **$7,800-$8,200**

KÄMMER & REINHARDT MORITZ
16" K(star)R bisque character 124 known as "Moritz." Blue "flirty" eyes and original wig. Dressed in felt, with K(star)R body. Also included, one book featuring Max and Moritz characters. Body has a re-glue at ankle, two broken fingers, some crazing, but retains original finish. . **$28,000-$30,000**

KÄMMER & REINHARDT MEIN LEIBLING
22" K(star)R 117 "Mein Leibling." Wearing an antique white cotton dress, brown boots, and a replacement brown human hair wig. Amber sleep eyes, clean bisque, on composition ball-jointed body. Very fine condition.
.... **$6,400-$7,000**

J. D. Kestner, after 1860

Though J. D. Kestner was founded in 1816 in Waltershausen, Germany, Kestner bisque dolls were introduced following the acquisition of a porcelain factory in 1860. Kestner produced complete dolls, and also supplied doll heads to other manufacturers.

The firm used various markings, including its name, initials, mold numbers, and a series of letters. "Excelsior" was a trade name of Kestner dolls distributed in the United States. The bisque head dolls may be found with various body types.

KESTNER BISQUE DOME HEAD
10" bisque dome head, marked "JDK, Made in Germany, Kestner," open/closed mouth, blue stationary eyes, composition body, wearing a white dotted Swiss-style dress.
.... **$800-$1,000**

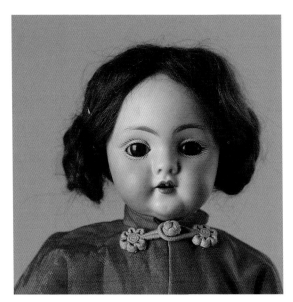

KESTNER GERMAN CHILD

12 1/2" German bisque Kestner 143 child. With brown sleep eyes, open mouth with two upper teeth, and fully jointed Kestner body. Brown mohair wig with coiled braids, in antique oriental costume. Original body finish. Overall excellent condition. ....$1,200-$1,500

KESTNER GIBSON GIRL

20" German bisque Kestner, known as "Gibson Girl," marked 172. Blue
sleep eyes, on a replaced leather body with composition lower limbs. Human
hair wig and a green silk two-piece walking suit. Some small peppering to
chin and side of nose. One or more hairlines to back of head with paint
touchup. "As is" condition..**$1,000-$1,500**

KESTNER CHARACTER BABY
20" German bisque Kestner character baby. Molded hair and brown sleep eyes. Open mouth with wobble tongue and two teeth. On a bent limb Kestner baby body and dressed in antique baby clothes. Body is in excellent original condition. Clothes are shredding. ....$1,600-$2,000

**KESTNER
SHOULDER HEAD
21" Kestner shoulder head**
marked "154." Blue sleep
eyes, open mouth with
teeth, kid body, wearing
an orange dress with ecru
lace, brown lace stockings,
leather shoes. .. **$600-$750**

KESTNER SHOULDER HEAD

Left, **22" Kestner bisque shoulder head,** marked "DEP 10154 Made in Germany," open mouth with teeth, brown stationary eyes, mint kid body, wearing a maroon silk dress and bonnet. Display ready condition.
....**$700-$850**

Right, **24" bisque head Karl Hartmann;** Karl Hartmann operated a doll factory and export business in Stockheim, Upper Franconia, Germany, from 1911 until 1926; marked with an "H" containing a small "K" in the upper section and a 4 in the lower section, replaced wig, open mouth with teeth, blue stationary eyes, jointed composition body, wearing a pink striped satin dress. .... **$700-$800**

KESTNER CLOSED-MOUTHED
24" closed-mouthed Kestner. Marked "15" on back of head, brown glass sleep eyes, and pale bisque. On an early chunky straight-wrist Kestner body. Blonde mohair wig, antique leather shoes and undergarments, and an aqua dress with black velvet trim with matching tam. Beautifully presented, display ready, good condition..**$3,800-$4,500**

KESTNER TURNED SHOULDER HEAD
26" Kestner turned shoulder head. Brown sleep eyes and pale bisque. On a replaced cloth body with bisque lower arms, wearing child's peach wool dress trimmed with blue braid, and children's boots with wooden heels. Wig is a blonde human hair replacement. Small pepper flake on chin. Lower legs are recovered. .... **$500-$600**

KESTNER BISQUE HEAD
30" bisque-head Kestner, marked "DEP-154 N," open mouth with teeth, brown sleep eyes, kid leather body, composition arms and hands, wearing an elaborate ecru dress and cap, replaced leather shoes. ....**$1,200-$1,400**

Kley & Hahn, founded 1902

Founded in Ohrdruf, Thüringia, Germany, by Albert Kley and Paul Hahn, the firm's specialty was making character dolls for the American market.

Several porcelain factories contributed to the Kley & Hahn inventory, including Bahr & Pröschild, Hertel, Schwab & Co., and Kestner.

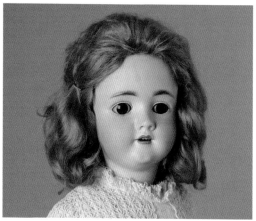

KLEY & HAHN WALKÜRE
29" German bisque Kley & Hahn "Walküre." Sandy blonde mohair wig, brown sleep eyes, on a fully jointed chunky German composition body, wearing an antique white windowpane and crochet child's dress. One finger re-glued, minor wear to joints. Head has crack from crown, down between eyes to left brow. "As is" condition... $300-$350

KLEY & HAHN
WALKÜRE
30" bisque Kley & Hahn "Walküre," marked "7 Germany Walküre," stationary threaded blue-gray eyes, open mouth with teeth, wearing a blue embroidered dress, old high-button shoes; body in fair condition, repaired crack behind head. "As is" condition.......... **$350-$400**
Perfect condition ....**$1,500-$1,700**

Gebrüder Kuhnlenz, founded 1884

Gebrüder Kuhnlenz was established by three brothers — Julius, Cuno, and Bruno — in Kronach, Bavaria.

GEBRÜDER KUHNLENZ BISQUE HEAD
8" bisque head, marked "G50K" in a sunburst and "44-17," blue stationary eyes, open mouth with teeth, composition body with hands made to hold a flag, wearing a navy suit and hat. .... **$300-$350**

GEBRÜDER KUHNLENZ SHOULDER HEAD LADY
20" German bisque G.K. 38-28 shoulder head lady. Blue paperweight eyes, pierced ears, and human hair wig. Solid dome head, kid body with bisque lower arms. Black scratch on right cheek, appears to have a right eye chip. Body has some patching at gussets. "As is" condition.................. **$300-$350**
If perfect ....$2,200-$2,600

A. Lanternier et Cie, founded 1855

This French firm located in Limoges began making doll heads in 1915. The quality of its work ranges from very good to coarse and grainy.

LANTERNIER CHARACTER BOY
20" French bisque character boy marked A-7. Lanternier, circa 1920. Blue paperweight eyes and open/closed mouth with two teeth and molded tongue. Blond mohair wig, on a French jointed composition body and redressed in Buster Brown costume. Small pepper marks on face, and hands are repainted. Some discoloration under right eye. .... **$1,400-$1,500**

A. G. Limbach, mid-19th century

The company that became A.G. Limbach was started by Gotthelf Greiner, near Alsbach, Thüringia, Germany. The Sonneberg, Germany, Museum has identified a china shoulder-head doll dating from 1850 as having been made by Limbach. Production of bisque doll heads was temporarily discontinued in 1899, resuming in 1919.

LIMBACH GERMAN BISQUE
14" German bisque doll marked with a cloverleaf on back of head. Brown paperweight eyes. Floral print cotton dress trimmed in red satin, original brimmed hat with feather on top, gauze underwear, black knit socks and oilcloth shoes. On a fully jointed straight-wrist body. Original short sandy blonde mohair wig. Body has original finish with very little wear.
.....................$1,200-$1,600

LIMBACH GIRL
22" German bisque Limbach girl is marked with cloverleaf on the back of head and "12." Blue paperweight eyes, open mouth with two square-cut teeth. On a straight-wrist fully jointed composition body. Human hair wig is a newer replacement, and new dress and hat are made in the French manner. Brown oilcloth shoes and white cotton underwear. Composition body has been repainted. Some peppering to right brow and tip of nose. "As is" condition. ....**$1,300-$1,500**

Armand Marseille, 1885 to 1930

Located in Sonneberg and Köppelsdorf, Thüringia, Germany, Armand Marseille was one of the largest suppliers of bisque doll heads in the world, reportedly producing a thousand heads a day.

Companies using Armand Marseille heads include Amberg, Arranbee, C. M. Bergmann, Borgfeldt, Butler Bros., Cuno & Otto Dressel, Eckart, Edelmann, Otto Gans, Goldberger, Hitz, Jacobs & Kassler, Illfelder, E. Maar, Montgomery Ward, Emil Pfeiffer, Peter Scherf, Seyfarth & Reinhardt, Siegel Cooper, E.U. Steiner, Wagner & Wetzsche, Wislizenus, and Louis Wolf & Co.

ARMAND MARSEILLE DOME-HEAD BABIES
8" bisque dome-head babies, marked "AM Germany 1440K," blue sleep eyes, closed mouths, wearing bunting. ....$300-$350 each

ARMAND MARSEILLE GOOGLY
9" German bisque A.M. 200 Googly. Five-piece body with side-glancing blue eyes. Human hair wig with newer clothes. Overall excellent, body somewhat dirty but retains original paint. ....$2,200-$2,700

**ARMAND
MARSEILLE
BISQUE HEAD**
11" bisque head,
marked "390 AM,"
sleep eyes, open
mouth with teeth,
composition body,
wearing a traditional
Dutch costume and
wooden shoes, all of
which are original.
.... **$300-$350**

ARMAND MARSEILLE BISQUE DOME HEAD
12" bisque dome head (8" circumference) baby, marked "Germany 341 AM," blue stationary eyes, closed mouth, cloth body, celluloid hands, wearing a long white dress. .... **$400-$450**

ARMAND MARSEILLE 1894 GIRL
12" German bisque A.M. 1894 girl, dressed in patriotic outfit representing "Miss Columbia." Retains original wig and shoes. Open mouth and four teeth, and fully jointed composition body. Some discoloration to right side of forehead, light scuffing on the arms, some wear and touch-up to knee joints. Fabric is weak on costume with overall soiling. Very appealing, display-ready, original condition. .... $500-$550

ARMAND MARSEILLE CHARACTER BABY
12" bisque head character baby, marked "AM 985," blue stationary eyes, open mouth with teeth, jointed baby body, wearing a white cotton dress.
....$500-$550

ARMAND MARSEILLE SCOWLING INDIAN
12 1/2" bisque head (Scowling Indian), marked "4/0 Armand Marseilles," open mouth with teeth, brown stationary eyes, composition body, wearing white leather outfit, beaded and fringed.
.... **$400-$450**

ARMAND MARSEILLE FANY

13" A.M. Fany #231. Blue glass sleep eyes, on straight wrist, short chunky body. Wearing a yellow cotton print dress and blonde mohair wig. Lacking shoes. Repainting to lower arms and thighs. Eye chip on doll's lower left rim by nose. "As is" condition. ....$3,500-$4,000
If perfect ....$7,500-$7,900

ARMAND MARSEILLE GOOGLY
13 1/2" German bisque A.M. 253 Googly. White eyelet and cloth shoes. Original blonde mohair wig and side-glancing brown sleep eyes. Minor wear. ....**$4,500-$4,700**

ARMAND MARSEILLE FLAPPER LADY
14" A.M. 401 flapper lady. With blue sleep eyes and brown mohair wig. Original underwear, stockings, and shoes, and a knit pink and white cotton dress with matching hat. Composition flapper style body. Lacking some fingertips on both hands, ball joints have paint chipping. .....**$1,600-$1,800**

ARMAND MARSEILLE BISQUE HEAD

14" bisque head, marked "Otto Gans/Germany 975/A 2 M/Seyfarth," open mouth with teeth, blonde wig, brown sleep eyes, composition body, wearing a white cotton dress with ruffles. .... **$500-$600**

ARMAND MARSEILLE BISQUE DOME HEAD

Left, **14" bisque dome head baby,** marked "AM Germany 341-13," baby open/close eyes, closed mouth, cloth body, celluloid hands, wearing a white cotton dress and sweater. .... **$550-$650**

Right, **14" bisque dome head,** marked "Baby Phyllis, Made in Germany," blue sleep eyes, closed mouth, cloth body, composition hands, wearing a white cotton dress. .... **$900-$1,000**

ARMAND MARSEILLE BISQUE BABY
14 1/2" German bisque A.M. GB 329 baby. Blue-gray sleep eyes, original blonde mohair wig. Five-piece baby body has original pink finish, wearing a pink checked romper and sweater set. Open mouth with two lower teeth. Two missing fingers on left hand, light wear to the finish on both hands, and chipping on toes. Left arm needs to be restrung. .... **$550-$600**

ARMAND MARSEILLE BISQUE HEAD
15" bisque head, marked "Made in Germany 390 AM," brown stationary eyes, open mouth with teeth, fully jointed composition toddler body, replaced wig, wearing a blue cotton dress. Exceptionally nice, soft coloring.
.... **$500-$550**

ARMAND MARSEILLE
18" Armand Marseille,
marked "AM 1894 2 DEP,"
brown stationary eyes,
open mouth with teeth,
jointed composition body,
wearing a white cotton and
crocheted dress. Nice coloring, feathered brows.
.... $450-$500

ARMAND MARSEILLE PAINTED BISQUE
19" painted bisque, marked "AM," blue sleep eyes, open mouth with teeth, molded braided hair over ears, jointed composition body, wearing a navy skirt and embroidered vest and blouse, and black and white leather shoes. Rarely found; good original condition. .... $600-$750

ARMAND MARSEILLE CHARACTER BABY
21" bisque head character baby, marked "Germany G 37 B, DRGM 259 A 9 M," blue sleep eyes, open mouth with teeth, jointed composition body, wearing a long white baby dress. ....,,.. **$700-$900**

**ARMAND MARSEILLE
SHOULDER HEAD**
22" bisque shoulder head, marked "AM 370," blue stationary eyes, open mouth with teeth, replaced brown wig, jointed kid body, nicely feathered brows, redressed in a two-piece tangerine-pink dress with ecru lace and matching hat. .... **$325-$350**

ARMAND MARSEILLE QUEEN LOUISE
24" bisque head, marked "Queen Louise, Made in Germany," blue threaded stationary eyes, open mouth with teeth, replaced wig, jointed composition body, redressed wearing an old dress of dark gold silk, 1920s style, with red trim and olive green sateen, new shoes.
.... $500-$600

**ARMAND MARSEILLE
SHOULDER HEAD**
**24" bisque shoulder
head,** marked "Germany
370 A3M Armand Mar-
seilles," blue sleep eyes,
open mouth with teeth,
blonde wig, kid body,
wearing a checked dress
with red satin trim, leather
shoes stitched on body.
.... $450-$500

ARMAND MARSEILLE SHOULDER HEAD
25" **A.M. 370.** Shoulder head, on a simulated kid body with cloth upper arms and lower bisque arms. Blue sleep eyes and mohair wig, dressed in a wool lady's jacket and skirt. Body has normal soiling and wear, tape at the shoulder plate, and two broken fingers. .... $500-$550

ARMAND MARSEILLE BISQUE HEAD
40" bisque head, marked "AM," brown stationary eyes, open mouth with teeth, replaced papier-mâché body parts, wearing a white girl's dress and leather shoes. ....**$2,000-$2,500**

May Freres, Cie., 1882 to 1901

May Freres, Cie. is known for making Mascotte Bébés. Records indicate that Jules Steiner purchased May Freres and advertised Bébé Mascotte after 1897, as did Jules Mettais, Steiner's 1899 successor.

MASCOTTE BÉBÉ
19" French bisque Mascotte Bébé. Closed mouth with blue paperweight eyes on a fully jointed composition body marked "BÉBÉ MASCOTTE." Retains some underwear and socks. Wig is a French human hair replacement. Body is in fine original condition with some scuffs and dirt to torso.
.... $4,500-$4,800

Alexandre Mothereau, 1880 to 1895

Solid information about Alexandre Celestin Triburee Mothereau is scarce. The French firm produced Bébé Mothereau for only about 15 years.

The bodies have turned-wooden upper limbs and rounded-joint lower limbs, with metal brackets to accept elastic stringing. They have long and thin torsos, and small hands and feet.

BÉBÉ MOTHEREAU
22" Bébé Mothereau. Marked on rear of head "B. 9 M." Brown threaded paperweight eyes, on a jointed French body. Wearing an embroidered brown French Bébé dress, human hair wig with braids covering each ear, and antique leather shoes. Couple black specks on face. .... **$27,000-$30,000**

BÉBÉ MOTHEREAU
28" Bébé Mothereau. With light brown threaded paperweight eyes with mauve eye shadowing. Original skin wig. Possibly original red cotton dress with black piping and marked French shoes. Rear of head is marked "B. 10 M." On French straight-wrist composition body. Overall condition is very fine. Rare.. $35,000-$38,000

Petit & Dumontier, 1878 to 1890

Petit & Dumontier was founded by Frederic Petit and Andre Dumontier, with some heads made by Francois Gaultier.

PETIT & DUMONTIER BÉBÉ
17" French P. 1. D. Petit & Dumontier Bébé. On a jointed composition body (incorrect) with blue paperweight eyes, dressed in white cotton dress with blue highlighting. Although head has had restoration, the facial details have not been affected. "As is" condition. .... **$3,000-$3,500**

PETIT & DUMONTIER BÉBÉ
18" French P. 2. D. Petit & Dumontier Bébé (circa 1880s) with dark brown paperweight eyes and some mauve eye shadowing. Pale bisque on a fully jointed composition body with metal hands. Dressed in an antique child's white cotton dress. Wearing antique shoes and socks. Sandy blonde human hair wig with curls, possibly replaced. Overall condition is very fine with normal wear to body at joints. Some paint loss to metal hands. Rare.
.... **$17,000-$21,000**

PETIT & DUMONTIER BÉBÉ

26" French P. 5 D. Petit & Dumontier Bébé with bulbous blue paperweight eyes, pale bisque, on the proper composition ball-jointed composition body with metal hands. Wearing antique velvet dress with shoulder cuffs and lace trim at shoulders (majority of velvet has dissipated) and white two-strap shoes. Replacement auburn human hair wig. Wear and flaking to lower arms and metal hands. .... **$30,000-$32,000**

**PETIT & DUMONTIER
26" French P. 5 D.** Large
almond-eye cut and blue
paperweight eyes. On a
jointed French style body
(not correct), wearing a
sea-foam green antique
dress, replaced human
hair wig and straw bonnet.
Body has been repainted,
nose has slight rub. "As is"
condition.
.... **$20,000-$22,000**

Pintel & Godchaux, 1887 to 1899

Based in Montreuil-sous-Bois, France, Pintel & Godchaux registered the trade name "Bébé Charmat" in 1892. They also received a patent for a body with a diagonal hip joint.

PINTEL & GODCHAUX BÉBÉ
24" French Pintel & Godchaux Bébé. Marked "P 11 G" on rear of head. Blue paperweight eyes, on a composition and wood French ball-jointed body, wearing a replica French outfit. Bisque has a few pimples: one on eyebrow and a couple on the cheek. ....$4,000-$4,600

PINTEL & GODCHAUX BÉBÉ
14" French bisque P.G. Bébé. Attributed to Pintel & Godchaux, on a fully jointed wood and composition body. Blue paperweight eyes with even bisque. Dressed in antique underwear and shoes with a replacement blonde human hair wig. Comes with newer French-style costume. Overall very good to excellent condition. ....**$2,500-$2,800**

Rabery & Delphieu, 1856 to 1899

A Paris manufacturer focusing on doll bodies, Rabery & Delphieu became part of the Societé Française de Fabrication de Bébés & Jouets in 1899. In the last quarter of the 19th century, Francois Gaultier supplied bisque heads and arms for Rabery & Delphieu Bébés. These were made using both pressed and poured bisque methods.

RABERY & DELPHIEU
15" Rabery & Delphieu. Brown paperweight eyes and uniform bisque. Marked "R 2/O D." On a jointed French composition body and wearing original factory chemise, with original French blonde mohair wig (sparse). Small damage to side of torso, probably where doll stand was placed on doll. "As is" condition with slight body damage. ....$3,000-$3,200

Theodor Recknagel, after 1893

Recknagel's porcelain factory in Alexandrienthal, Thüringia, Germany, was founded in 1886, but there is no evidence of doll production before 1893, when he registered two tinted Mulatto doll heads.

RECKNAGEL BISQUE HEADS

Left, **9 1/2" bisque shoulder head,** marked "1907," open mouth with teeth, black glass eyes, fabric legs, old white cotton dress with lace. **$175-$225**

Right, **6 1/2" bisque head girl,** marked "1909 DEP R 0/0 A, Recknagel of Germany," papier-mâché body (stamped "I can close my eyes – Made in Germany"), blonde mohair wig, blue sleep eyes, open mouth with teeth, wearing a white cotton dress. Finding an original doll with evidence of its history is always desirable. ..**$300-$350** Without original interesting factory dress ....**$100-$150**

Mme. Rohmer, 1857 to 1880

Marie Antoinette Leontine Rohmer of Paris produced dolls in both china and bisque. She obtained several patents for improvements to doll bodies. The first, for articulated kid body joints, was followed by a patent for gutta percha or rubber doll arms. Another patent was for a new type of doll's head with a cord running through it into the body and out riveted holes in the front of the torso. This allowed turning of the head in any direction and also secured the head to the body.

ROHMER FASHION
18" Rohmer fashion. "Cup and saucer" neck on a marked kid body. Bisque arms attached to the leather upper, which swivel at the shoulder. Pale bisque, blue eyes. Wearing a striped blue and white wool outfit, black leather boots and a cotton blouse with blue piping, a (possibly original) sandy blonde human hair wig, and a felt pillbox hat with velvet leaf attachments. Outfit has some moth damage. Beautiful doll in apparently good condition.
......................................$7,900-$8,400

Bruno Schmidt, founded 1900

Located in Waltershausen, Germany, records indicate that Bruno Schmidt's character bisque heads were purchased exclusively from Bähr & Pröschild, which Bruno Schmidt eventually acquired.

BRUNO SCHMIDT WENDY

11" German bisque Bruno Schmidt 537 character known as "Wendy." Rare petite version of this doll. Original blonde mohair wig. Antique, possibly original clothes. Antique leather shoes marked with a "2." Light pepper on cheek. Light wear to body, one fingertip is missing. Apparently excellent condition...**$15,000-$17,500**

Schmitt et Fils, 1863 to 1891

The French firm of Schmitt et Fils was located at Nogent-sur-Marne, Seine, and Paris.

Schmitt et Fils Bébés usually are made using pressed, rather than poured, bisque. Wax and wax-over papier-mâché examples also have been found. They are typically marked "SCH" with crossed hammers within a shield. (Also see papier-mâché and wax.)

SCHMITT BÉBÉ
15" Schmitt Bébé. Threaded blue eyes, pale bisque, fully jointed body marked Schmitt. Wearing antique shoes, underwear, blonde mohair wig, and French skirt and jacket with matching hat. Marked on the rear of head with the Schmitt shield and a "0" below, original composition pate is also marked with shield and a "0." Composition body has normal wear at joints although torso shows crazing to composition. A few minor wig chips to side and rear of head. Small pepper mark on doll's left cheek. ...**$20,000-$22,000**

SCHMITT BÉBÉ

24" Schmitt Bébé. Blue paperweight eyes. Wearing an antique white cotton dress with lace trim, lace bonnet, and sandy blonde mohair wig. On a marked Schmitt body. White pinprick flake on lower cheek and a hairline extends toward chin continuing up towards nose. "As is" condition.

....$10,000-$14,000

If perfect ....$32,000-$33,000

Schmitt Bébé
25" Schmitt Bébé. Pale bisque, blue threaded paperweight eyes with mauve eye-shadowing. Wearing an antique silk cream dress with a silk ribbon trim throughout and a blonde mohair wig. On a Schmitt body (repainted). One brown pinprick speck between eyebrows.
.... $22,000-$26,000

Schoenau & Hoffmeister, 1901 to 1953

Located in Burggrub, Bayern, Germany, the Schoenau & Hoffmeister factory produced bisque doll heads in both the shoulder head and socket head types.

SCHOENAU & HOFFMEISTER BABY GIRL
7 1/2" bisque head baby girl, marked "S*H Hanna 12 1/2 Schoenau & Hoffmeister of Bavaria, Germany," excellent composition jointed body, brown sleep eyes, open mouth with teeth, wearing a white romper.
....$400-$500

SCHOENAU & HOFFMEISTER BISQUE HEAD
13" bisque head, marked "S*H PB (in star), Schoenman & Porzellanfabrik Burggrub," blue stationary eyes, open mouth with teeth, replaced wig, stick body (probably replaced), redressed wearing a cream-colored dress with pearls. "As is" condition... **$200-$250**

SCHOENAU & HOFFMEISTER BISQUE HEAD

20" bisque head, marked "BP 5859 Germany," blue threaded sleep eyes, open mouth with teeth, jointed composition baby body, redressed wearing a maroon velvet dress and hat with lace. .... **$600-$700**

SCHOENAU & HOFFMEISTER BISQUE HEAD
25" bisque head, marked "S*H 1909 Schoenman & Porzellanfabrik Burggrub," open mouth with teeth, brown sleep eyes, composition body, redressed wearing a yellow silk dress, new shoes. .... **$500-$600**

SCHOENAU & HOFFMEISTER GERMAN CHILD
29" German bisque Schoenau Hoffmeister 5800 child. Brown sleep eyes and original silk lashes. On a fully jointed German composition body, wearing a scarlet sailor suit and red oilcloth shoes. Brown human hair wig and black velvet cap. Body has repair to fingers and repaint to hands and feet, and minute flake to corner of right eye. "As is" condition, but visually appealing and beautifully costumed. .... **$800-$900**
If perfect .... **$1,500-$1,700**

Simon & Halbig, after 1860

Located in Graefenhain and Hildburghausen, near Ohrdruf, Thüringia, Germany, Simon & Halbig made tinted and untinted bisque shoulder heads. Varieties include solid dome, open pate or Belton-Type; molded and painted hair or wigged; painted, stationary, sleep paperweight or flirty eyes; open, closed, or open/closed mouths; and pierced or unpierced ears.

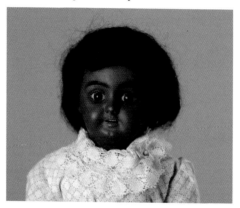

SIMON & HALBIG GERMAN CHILD
11 1/2" German brown bisque Simon & Halbig 739 child. Original chocolate brown fully jointed composition body. Brown set eyes and open mouth with four teeth. Newly dressed in blue and white cotton with new shoes, but still retains original black mohair wig, which has never been removed. Wear at neck socket where there appears to be some re-gluing to shoulder seams. ....**$1,400-$1,600**

SIMON & HALBIG BLACK CHARACTER
14" black S&H 1368 character. With open mouth, dressed in ethnic costume on a jointed French composition body. Wearing original nappy hair wig, with set light brown paperweight eyes. Antique clothing and shoes. Body overall is fine with minor wear to fingertips and at joints. Beautifully preserved, rare doll in very good to excellent condition. ....$7,000-$7,500

SIMON & HALBIG FLAPPER LADY
14" Simon & Halbig 1469 flapper lady. Gray-blue eyes, flawless bisque, original bobbed blonde mohair wig. Costumed in 1920s style gauze wedding dress and net veil. White leather replacement slippers, long silk stockings, and a bouquet of cloth flowers. Minute flaking at neck socket and some fine crazing to upper legs. Lovely doll in appealing costume.........$3,700-$4,400

SIMON & HALBIG ORIENTAL
15" Simon & Halbig 1329 Oriental. Even skin coloring, original black mohair wig, and costumed in oriental fabrics. On a jointed German composition body with proper Oriental tinting. ....$3,000-$3,200

SIMON & HALBIG SHOULDER HEAD
16" bisque shoulder head, marked "Simon Halbig," pierced ears, brown stationary eyes, open mouth with teeth, redressed wearing a lace wedding dress, visually appealing, seemingly good condition. .... **$800-$950**

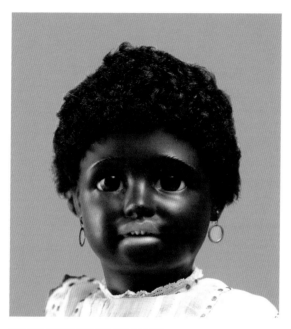

SIMON & HALBIG BLACK CHARACTER
22" black S&H 1358 character. Brown set eyes on a jointed composition body. Wearing an antique white cotton dress with red polka dots, antique leather shoes, and an older curly black mohair wig. Minor wear at joints. Rare. Seemingly in very good to excellent condition.......... **$25,000-$28,000**

SIMON & HALBIG LADY
25" German bisque Simon & Halbig lady doll, mold 1159. Blue paperweight eyes, blonde mohair wig, and full-figured Simon & Halbig lady body. Frail maroon dress, possibly original. Normal wear to joints. Shoes are newer replacements. ....$3,200-$3,700

SIMON & HALBIG SHOULDER HEAD

26" bisque shoulder head, marked "S&H, DEP, Simon Halbig 1009," dark brown sleep eyes, open mouth with teeth, pierced ears, kid body, wearing a brown dress and hat.

.... **$1,200-$1,400**

SIMON & HALBIG LADY

26 1/2" German bisque S&H 1079 lady. On appropriate lady body, dressed in antique Gibson-style dress with human hair wig. Hairlines to side of face. Eyes have been glued in, but are now loose in head. Body retains its original finish with wear to hands. "As is" condition..............................**$1,200-$1,500**

Note: Value of parts:

Rare lady body .... $700-$800

Human hair wig.. $100-$150

Vintage dress .... $250-$300

Damaged head .... $150-$250

SIMON & HALBIG SWIVEL HEAD

28" bisque swivel head on deep bisque shoulder plate, marked "S12H 1009 DEP, Simon Halbig" (slight scratch on cheek), blue threaded paperweight eyes, open mouth with teeth, blonde wig, kid body, bisque lade lower arms, redressed wearing a green and black dress with black hat.
........................**$1,400-$1,500**

SIMON & HALBIG BROWN GIRL
20" German bisque brown S&H 1039 girl. Large brown stationary eyes, long human hair wig, and is on a fully jointed German body. Antique red dress with a later corduroy coat and hat. Fine scuffing to cheeks, teeth are chipped, and body is repainted. "As is" condition. .... $850-$1,000
If perfect .... $1,400-$1,700

Societé Française de Fabrication de Bébés & Jouets

The Societé Française de Fabrication de Bébés & Jouets, or French Society for the Manufacture of Bébés and Toys, is commonly referred to as S.F.B.J. In 1899, the society signed an agreement for locations in Paris and Montreuil-sous-Bois, France, establishing a syndicate to compete with German manufacturers.

Most of the best-known French firms joined the S.F.B.J. and continued to produce the same dolls that they had made as individual companies. Because so many different porcelain factories—using different molds—were involved, the quality of the products varies widely.

Two types of dolls were produced by S.F.B.J.: the familiar bébés and character dolls. The characters were modeled after real children with portrait-like detail as opposed to the idealized "dolly face" bébé. They were pouting, laughing, screaming, or smiling, as they portrayed baby or adolescent.

S.F.B.J. GOOGLY
8" French bisque S.F.B.J. 245 Googly. Fully jointed composition body. Blue side-glancing stationary eyes. Newer blue and white mariner's costume. Red mohair wig and newer shoes. Slight ruddiness to bisque. Body in original paint. .... **$4,000-$4,500**

S.F.B.J. CHARACTER BOX
S.F.B.J. French character box. Consisting of one complete doll (13 1/2") and two additional character heads with change of clothing in original display box. The mold numbers of the three dolls are: 237, 235, and 233. All have glass paperweight eyes and flocked hair. Lid of box has description in three languages of "The new interchangeable doll. Simple, clever and amusing." Box size: 19" by 14 1/2". The 235 and 237 characters have inherent factory mold lines at base of neck. Some minor paint flaking to composition ball-jointed body. Pristine, near mint condition. .... **$14,000-$16,000/set**

S.F.B.J. CHARACTER TODDLER

14" French bisque S.F.B.J. 247 character toddler. Blue sleep eyes, open/closed mouth with two molded teeth on a jointed French toddler body. Dressed in a two-piece corduroy boy's suit with new human hair wig and replaced shoes. Hands are flaking with normal wear to rest of body. Light scuffing on cheeks and upper lip. ....$1,900-$2,100

S.F.B.J. FRENCH BISQUE
15" French bisque S.F.B.J. 301. Dressed as a lady in black striped cotton.
Original human hair wig and pate. On a jointed French composition body,
wearing newer black and white leather shoes. Brown sleep eyes with some
wax missing on the lids. Hands may have been replaced. .... **$700-$800**

S.F.B.J. CHARACTER BABY
16" French bisque S.F.B.J. 236 character baby. Two molded teeth, brown sleep eyes, and brown mohair wig. Dressed in an older mariner's costume with newer shoes. On a five-piece S.F.B.J. baby body. Body has repair to fingers. $1,200-1,400

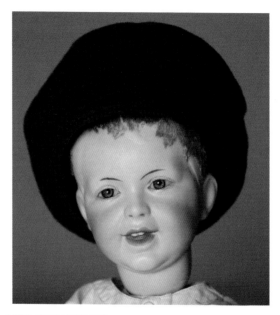

S.F.B.J. CHARACTER BOY
17" French S.F.B.J. 235 character boy with original box. Blue jeweled eyes with strawberry-blonde flocked hair (some loss to flocking), well molded facial features and fine bisque. Wearing original marked "AU BON MARCHE" shoes, on a jointed composition body. Original clothing (perhaps lacking coat) and an extra nightshirt. Near mint condition, with box. ....$3,800-$4,000

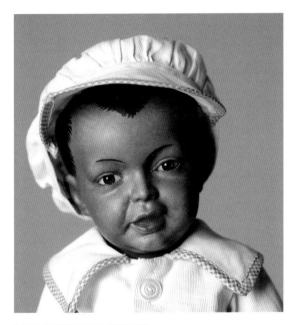

S.F.B.J. BROWN CHARACTER BOY
17" French bisque S.F.B.J. 226 brown character boy. Painted hair and glass paperweight eyes and molded open/closed mouth. On a brown jointed French composition body and dressed in a three-piece boy's white and blue costume with antique oilcloth shoes. Body repainted ....**$2,400-$2,600**

S.F.B.J. CHARACTER TODDLER
19" S.F.B.J. 252 character toddler. Wearing an antique gauze style dress with hat. Blue glass sleep eyes and a newer blonde curly mohair wig. Rear of head is marked "252." Wearing marked S.F.B.J. shoes marked "9." Body condition overall is very good with minor paint touch-up. ...**$5,200-$5,500**

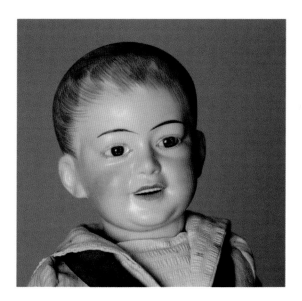

S.F.B.J. CHARACTER BOY
19" S.F.B.J. 227 character boy. Molded and painted hair with open mouth and teeth, blue jeweled eyes on a fully jointed French composition body (hands repainted). Wearing original sailor outfit (shoes replaced). Even, softly colored bisque socket head marked "227." Hairline to left side coming out of neck socket and extending 3" up to outside corner of eye. Old repair evident but not visible when doll is on display. "As is" condition.
.... **$900-$1,400**
If perfect ....$2,600-$2,800

S.F.B.J. CHARACTER BOY
21" French bisque S.F.B.J. 233 character boy. On a jointed French body and dressed in a boy's two-piece red, white, and blue wool costume. Restoration to back of neck. Body retains original finish except repainting to hands. "As is" condition. ....$1,800-$2,100
If perfect ....$5,900-$6,200

Hermann Steiner, after 1920

The factories of Hermann Steiner were located in Sonneberg, Neustadt, Thüringia, Germany, and in Bavaria. Although the company was founded in 1911, it did not produce dolls until 1920. This explains why the majority of dolls found with the Hermann Steiner mark are the character baby type, which was so popular and dominated the market at that time. Hermann Steiner had poor timing regarding the manufacture of bisque dolls, entering the market at the end of the era.

HERMANN STEINER DOME HEAD BOY
14" bisque dome head boy, marked with an "S" inside an "H", intaglio painted blue eyes, closed mouth, old stick body, wearing a navy wool suit, replaced shoes. ....**$500-$550**

Jules Steiner, founded 1855

Based in Paris, the Jules Steiner company was founded in 1855. Many Steiner dolls are marked with the name "Bourgoin," a Paris merchant dealing in porcelains and associated with Jules Steiner during the 1880s. Sometime after 1897, Steiner purchased May Freres, Cie., the company responsible for the manufacture of the Bébé Mascotte.

There is evidence that Steiner pressed its bisque doll heads even after other French manufacturers were routinely using the poured bisque method. Steiner Bébés have been found in sizes ranging from 8 1/2" to 38".

JULES STEINER BÉBÉ WITH TRUNK
8" Steiner A Bébé with trunk. Original satin dress with blonde mohair wig and gauze hat. Trunk contains original clothing plus newer additions. On a five-piece composition body. Overall condition very fine.
.... **$4,500-$4,800/set**

JULES STEINER BLACK BÉBÉ
14" black open mouth Steiner A7 Bébé. On a fully jointed Steiner body with golden brown paperweight eyes, and original pate and knappy hair wig. Wearing an original lace and ribbon dress (dress has paper tag inside), and has a beaded necklace. Slight rub to tip of nose. Rare, original condition.
.... **$3,600-$3,800**

JULES STEINER BÉBÉ

17" Steiner series "C" Bébé. With dark brown paperweight eyes, mauve eye shadowing and expressive face. On a straight-wrist, jointed, composition Steiner body. Clothing and wig (sparse) are original and the shoes are antique. One wrist shows wear due to bracelet. Minute white scuff on left side of doll's cheek. ....$5,200-$5,700

JULES STEINER A13
20" Steiner A13, on a marked straight-wrist Steiner body. Dark brown human hair wig, wearing an off-white dress. Body has been over-glazed/painted but still retains original Steiner stamp on hip. ....**$4,800-$5,200**

JULES STEINER BÉBÉ

21" Steiner A13 Bébé. Blue paperweight eyes, on a straight-wrist marked Steiner body with voice box. Wearing an ivory low-waisted blue and white eyelet dress, with antique leather shoes and a French human hair wig. Very fine condition. ....**$6,700-$7,100**

JULES STEINER BÉBÉ SERIES C
23" Steiner Bébé Series C. Blue paperweight eyes, slight mauve shadowing. Wearing a white and blue eyelet dress, and an older replacement human hair wig and original cardboard pate. Body appears to be an old repaint. ....**$7,000-$7,400**

JULES STEINER SERIES G
24" Steiner Series "G." With bisque, wire eyes on marked straight-wrist
Steiner body. Short blonde skin wig (replaced). Wearing antique cotton
blue/gray dress with pinstripes, leather shoes, and velvet hat. Hairlines to
bisque head and small eye chip on lower rim of left eye.
"As is" condition. .... $10,000-$11,000
If perfect .... $36,000-$37,000

JULES STEINER FIRE
25" Steiner Fire A15. With blue paperweight eyes and even complexion on a marked Steiner body. Wearing an antique silk dress, leather shoes, and a sandy human hair wig. Overall body is very good with some wear or minor touch-up. There are two pinprick black spots on tip of nose and a small black mark on forehead. ....$7,600-$8,000

JULES STEINER A19

28" A19 Steiner. Blue paperweight eyes, on a marked Steiner body. Wearing a frail antique child's dress with matching bonnet and a replacement human hair wig. Some wear to joints. Lower arms and hands have been repainted. Restoration to forehead does not involve facial features. ....**$4,500-$4,800**
If perfect .... $10,000-$12,000

Swaine & Co., after 1910

Robert Swaine's porcelain factory in Hüttensteinach, near Sonneberg, Germany, produced dolls for only a short period of time. Swaine dolls have a green ink "GESTCHUTZT GERMANY S & Co." stamp, in addition to incised marks.

SWAINE & CO. CHARACTER GIRL
15" B.P. character girl by Swaine. Intaglio eyes, on a jointed composition body (hands repainted) and wearing regional clothing with a black floss wig. Rub marks on cheeks and nose, and some speckling to bisque. Rare, beautifully presented, display ready condition. ...... $6,000-$7,000

A. Thuillier, active 1875 to 1893

A. Thuillier is also known by the initialed mark "A.T." François Gaultier provided at least some of the bisque heads used by Thuillier of Paris.

THUILLIER BÉBÉ
13" A. 3 T. Bébé.
Brown paperweight eyes on a kid body with bisque lower arms. Marked on head and shoulder plate. Wearing an elaborate white cotton dress with lace trim and matching bonnet, highlighted by aqua ribbons on dress and hat. Antique leather shoes and sandy blonde mohair wig. Thumb repaired on right hand. Rare. Very good condition, early A.T.
.... $40,000-$43,000

THUILLIER FRENCH BÉBÉ
16" French Bébé "A. 5 T." with bulbous blue paperweight eyes and well-defined molding. On a Bru body with a Bru shoulder plate (Bru Jne #4). Wearing a blonde mohair wig with a cream satin dress highlighted with silk netting and antique boots. Repair to crack from neck socket going up through cheek to eye and continuing up to crown, restoration to right side of face. Rare. "As is" condition.. **$8,000-$10,000**

THUILLIER BÉBÉ

17" A. Thuillier Bébé. Bulbous blue threaded paperweight eyes, fine modeling. Marked "A. 6 T." on rear of head. Straight-wrist, eight ball-jointed body. Wearing antique shoes and chemise. Beautiful, rare doll in very good condition. .... **$45,000-$47,000**

THUILLIER BÉBÉ
19" A. Thuillier Bébé. Marked on rear of head "A. 8 T.," on a proper style straight-wrist composition French body. Blue threaded paperweight eyes, antique shoes, underwear, and blonde mohair wig. Wearing a peach-colored two-piece satin dress with some deterioration to fabric. Paint restoration to head, but does not involve any of the facial features.
"As is" condition. .... **$12,000-$14,000**

THUILLIER BÉBÉ
**23 1/2" French A. 15
Thuillier Bébé.** On a French
jointed composition body.
Pale bisque with mauve eye
shadow is accentuated by her
bulbous blue paperweight
eyes (reset). Wearing a brown
bébé dress with matching hat,
antique French shoes and
socks, with leather gloves.
Ash blonde mohair wig with
shoulder-length curls. Body,
although French, is not proper
for this doll.
"As is" condition.
.... **$40,000-$45,000**
If perfect ....**$70,000-$72,000**

Van Rozen, active 1910 to 1914

A noted Belgian sculptor, J. Van Rozen designed doll heads in Paris. Her dolls are so rare that it is believed she created them as special commissions.

Van Rozen dolls are pressed, not poured, bisque, and are well marked with the Van Rozen name.

VAN ROZEN BLACK CHARACTER BOY
19" black smiling Van Rozen character boy. Dressed as a marquis and has marked French shoes (with bumblebee) and is wearing a white powder human hair wig and a three-cornered hat. Fully marked on rear of head "VAN ROZEN, FRANCE DEPOSE." Open lips exposing molded teeth. Inset dark brown eyes that are highlighted with painted black eyelashes. Overall body condition fine, minor chipping at elbows and one finger has been repaired. Rare doll in extremely fine condition with elaborate costume, display ready.
.... **$25,000-$27,000**

Adolf Wislizenus, after 1878

Adolf Wislizenus became sole owner in 1878 of a doll and toy factory that had been founded in 1851 in Waltershausen, Germany. After several ownership changes, the factory went out of business in 1931, and was acquired by König & Wernicke. Bähr & Pröschild, Simon & Halbig, and (after 1910) Ernst Heubach supplied bisque heads for A. Wislizenus dolls.

ADOLF WISLIZENUS SPECIAL
23" German bisque A.W. Special. Brown sleep eyes, human hair wig (appears replaced), redressed in the Gibson Girl manner. On a fully jointed German body. Very good condition. .... $700-$800

CHINA-HEAD DOLLS, 1840 TO 1940S

China heads of glazed porcelain were made primarily in Germany from 1840 to the 1940s. Identifying china heads according to manufacturer is nearly impossible. Facial features vary little. China heads characteristically have painted blue eyes; a red line, indicating eyelids; full cheeks; and a small, closed, smiling mouth.

Very rare early china heads were attached to commercially made jointed, wooden bodies with china limbs. Most china heads, however, were sold separately. The consumer either purchased a body or made one.

Several terms are used to describe china heads. The most commonly found models are named for their hairstyle. Occasionally, unique characteristics suggest additional classification. Glass-eyed china head dolls are referred to as "French china." Flesh-colored or pink luster china heads with wigs, rather than painted hair, are known as "English china." "Kinderkopf" is applied to any style of china head representing a child. A "china socket"-style head attached to a china shoulder plate is very rare and desirable.

Familiar to collectors are the "Pet Name" dolls with painted gold letters across the molded yoke. They gave a final, but short-lived, boost to the china head market until permanently losing ground to the lovely bisque dolls around the turn of the century.

Germany continued to produce china heads through the 1940s, and thereafter in other countries. Reproduction and modern china heads are plentiful and can be difficult to spot. Most are unmarked, making authentication that much more difficult. Although reproductions are very similar in appearance to the originals, some differences are evident. Reproductions usually have a good, clean slip, whereas it is common to find tiny black flecks called peppering in antique china heads. Antique china heads usually have a red line above the eyes, a characteristic often overlooked on a reproduction. Obtaining the doll's history or provenance would, of course, also be helpful.

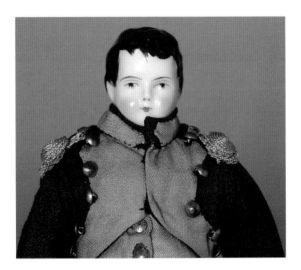

CHINA HEAD BOY
11" German china boy. Painted molded hair, blue painted eyes. On a kid body dressed in a handmade soldier's costume and wearing new leather shoes. Overall excellent condition. ....$1,200-$1,300

CHINA SHOULDER HEADS & "PET NAMES"
From left: 11" china shoulder head (broken at neck), black molded hair, blue sleep eyes, bisque hands and legs, painted shoes, cloth body, wearing a pink dress. "As is" condition. ....**$50-$60**
13" china shoulder head "pet name," marked "Bertha" on shoulder plate in raised gold lettering, black molded hair, "kidolene" body, bisque hands, wearing a cream-colored dress. ....**$200-$250**
12" china shoulder head "pet name," marked "Marian" on shoulder plate in raised gold lettering, cloth body stuffed with excelsior, china hands and lower legs, wearing a rose-colored dress. ....**$250-$275**

CHINA HEAD LADY
13" French china lady. Blue painted eyes. On a French kid body, with braided mohair wig, and dressed in an older two-piece blue and gray iridescent silk costume, and antique underwear. Body appears to be in sturdy condition with some soiling. ....$3,500-$3,800

CHINA SHOULDER HEAD
14" china shoulder head (firing flaw on nose, head has been repaired), kid body, bisque hands, wearing a peach-colored dress. "As is" condition.
....$25-$50

GERMAN CHINA HEAD
15" German china, 1850s "covered-wagon" style doll. On cloth body with china limbs, fine painting, and pale blue eyes. Redressed in a handmade blue silk dress with lace trim. Small pepper mark on the tip of nose, upper portion of body and limbs appear to be antique, but cloth portion of legs are new. Exceptionally nice example. "As is" condition. .... **$600-$800**

CHINA DRESSEL AND KISTER MAN
15" German china Dressel and Kister man. Detailed wavy gray/brown hair and brows. On a newer cloth and leather body and costumed in newer fabrics. Replacement body seems sturdy. "As is" condition. ..**$1,400-$1,500**
If perfect ....**$1,900-$2,200**

FRENCH CHINA POUPÈE
15" French china Poupèe. Blue glass eyes, fine detailing to lashes and brows. Original sparse skin wig, on a leather French body. Wearing a hand-sewn two-piece cotton floral dress and newer straw hat. Small pepper mark near right brow. ....$4,000-$4,500

CHINA DRESSEL AND KISTER LADY

15 1/2" German china Dressel and Kister lady. Painted gray hair and brows. On a cloth body with china limbs. Dressed in an ivory velvet two-piece gown. Shoulder plate needs to be sewn in place. Cloth body is of more recent vintage than head and limbs. "As is" condition............**$1,200-$1,400**
If perfect ....**$1,800-$2,300**

KPM CHINA HEAD MAN
16 1/2" KPM German china man (Krister Porzellan Manufaktur AG, Bavaria, founded 1831). Highly molded hair and fine facial detailing. On a cloth body with leather arms and wears shirt and pants. Shoulder plate is extensively restored but does not show above collar. Body is a newer replacement. "As is" condition. .... $600-$800

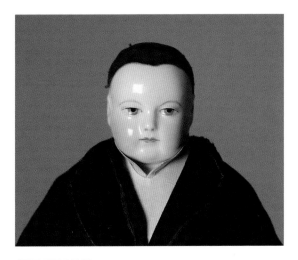

CHINA HEAD MAN
16 1/2" French china man. Molded eyelids, pale gray-blue painted eyes, and fine detail to lashes and brows. Kid body dressed in antique man's suit with "Boston" rubbers for shoes; wig missing. Overall excellent condition.
.... $4,400-$5,300

CHINA HEAD LADY
17" French china lady. Human hair wig and blue painted eyes. On a kid body with antique eyelet two-piece dress with red wool cape-style coat with featherstitch detailing and antique white leather boots. Body has some repairs to arms and overall normal wear and soiling. Fine hairline approximately 1/2" going from crown towards right eyebrow. "As is" condition. ....$800-$1,000

CHINA HEAD POUPÈE
17" French glass-eye china Poupèe, with eyeliner to top and bottom eyelids. In original frail costume with a letter of provenance stating that she was a Paris doll brought from Paris in 1860. On a sturdy body missing shoes and wig. Even glaze with one pit on left lower cheek. Beautiful example of an early rare French china head with glass eyes and provenance. .... **$6,000-$8,000**

Without provenance ....$4,500-$5,000

CHINA SHOULDER HEAD

17" china shoulder head (broken shoulder plate), blonde molded hair, blue eyes, cloth body, wearing a navy silk dress with lace collar. "As is" condition.. **$100-$125**

CHINA HEAD LADY
18" KPM German china lady with molded bun and exposed ears. On an old cloth body with red leather arms, wearing a red-checked homespun dress and original red leather slippers. Marked with a "7" on the back of her shoulder plate. Head has been reattached to body at some point. Firing crack at stringing hole on shoulder plate and another coming down to meet it, neither are visible when dressed. Minor scuffing to hair, cheek, and forehead. Body is in good condition. "As is" condition...........**$3,000-$3,200**

CHINA HEAD LADY
19" KPM German china lady. Brown molded hair pulled back in bun. On a cloth body wearing a pink silk fashion dress with train. Small white spot on tip of nose and very light speckling on left cheek. Body is weak and needs repair. Fading to front of dress. ....**$6,500-$7,000**

CHINA "MORNING GLORY"
20" German china known as "Morning Glory." Braided molded bun with molded flower detailing behind each ear and blue eyes. On an old cloth body with china limbs, dressed in antique cotton fabrics and antique underwear. Shoulder plate is extensively repaired, and repair has yellowed. Costume has light soiling on sleeves, and body has overall soiling with some repair.

.... $2,500-$3,000

If perfect ....,,,,,......................... $9,000-$10,000

CHINA HEAD LADY

21" German china lady, with brown eyes, 1860s molded black hairdo, on old cloth body with leather limbs. Dressed in an antique blue and brown cotton dress and antique underwear. Several small pepper marks to right side of face, minor scuffing on the hair in front and back. Leather limbs are in poor condition and left hand is missing. Stitched-on leather boots are missing the toes. ....**$1,200-$1,400**
If perfect ....**$1,800-$2,000**

PINK-TINT CHINA HEAD LADY

22" English pink-tint china lady. Antique mohair wig and long slender arms. Body is cloth with china limbs, wearing a newer peach velvet two-piece costume. Light speckling to face, deep pit center of forehead under the wig. Right thumb has been broken and re-glued, right bisque leg is restored and repainted. New cloth body in sturdy condition. ....$2,000-$2,200
If perfect ....$3,800-$4,000

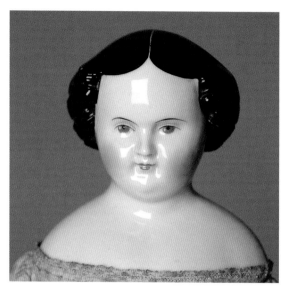

CHINA HEAD LADY
24" German china lady, with brown eyes. 1860s, black hair with fine
painting detail. On cloth body with china limbs. Original muslin dress and
underwear. Lower right china leg has been broken and re-glued. Dress is
soiled. ....**$1,000-$1,200**
If perfect ....**$1,200-$1,450**

CHINA SHOULDER HEAD
25" china shoulder head, blue eyes, black molded hair (firing flaw on chin), old cloth body, leather hands and sewed-on leather shoes, wearing a black silk dress with shawl. .... $500-$600

CHINA HEAD
28" china head, blue eyes, cloth body, leather hands and shoes, dressed in olive green wool with black braid trim (back of shoulder plate broken). ....**$800-$1,100**
If perfect ....**$2,200-$2,400**

31" china head, original cloth body, leather hands, blue eyes, black hair, wearing a period brown cotton plaid dress with leather shoes that do not match. The mismatched shoes add to the doll's charm and visual appeal.
....**$1,200-$1,400**

CHINA SHOULDER HEAD BOY
33" china shoulder head boy, black molded hair, blue eyes, old cloth body, leather shoes and hands, wearing a black suit. ....$2,500-$3,000

PARIAN-HEAD DOLLS

First used in the mid-19th century, parian is a creamy-white, slightly translucent porcelain, deliberately designed to look like the fine marble from the Greek island of Paros, which was used in classical times for important statues.

Various German porcelain factories produced parian dolls from the late 1850s through the early 1880s, and Parian has become a generic term for the pale or untinted bisque dolls of the 19th century. Some may bear a number code, but most are unmarked.

PARIAN "DOLLY MADISON" TYPE
18" German Parian with molded hair. A "Dolly Madison" type with blue molded hair ribbon, painted and decorated shoulder plate, and blue painted eyes. On a cloth body with older replacement cotton dress. Hands missing, lower legs in fragile, poor condition..$1,100-$1,200
If perfect ....$1,400-$1,500

PARIAN MAN

21" German Parian man with molded shoulder plate. Shoulder plate has molded blue polka-dot tie with gold highlighting. On cloth body with leather arms, wearing a man's suit and antique oilcloth shoes. Costume is frail, body and hands are sturdy. ....$2,500-$2,700

PARIAN SHOULDER HEAD
23" Parian shoulder head, blonde molded hair, cloth body, bisque hands and feet, wearing a gold velvet dress. ....,.............**$1,000-$1,200**

Synthetic Materials: Celluloid, Hard Plastic, Latex, Rubber, Vinyl

Though this category covers a wide range of materials used for doll manufacture—starting in the second half of the 19th century and continuing today—all of these man-made products have one thing in common: Each was an attempt to make dolls faster, cheaper, more realistic, and longer lasting. As you will see, the results—especially regarding durability—are mixed.

CELLULOID

Celluloid is a brittle, flammable thermoplastic composed mainly of cellulose nitrate and camphor.

Originally a trademark, celluloid was produced in Europe, the United States, Japan, and other countries from the late 1860s until about 1950. Many companies produced celluloid dolls or celluloid doll parts, including Le Minor, Parsons Jackson, Kämmer & Reinhardt, Petitcollin, Kestner, Averill, Irwin, Marks, and Rheinische Gummi, which claimed it was the first to manufacture celluloid dolls.

Marks include an embossed stork (Parsons-Jackson), turtle (Schultz), Indian head (American), mermaid (Cellba), beetle or ladybug (Hernsdorfer-Germany), star (Hollywood), SNF (Société Nobel Francaise), ASK (Zast of Poland). For additional marks, refer to *Antique Trader's Doll Makers and Marks* by Dawn Herlocher.

In 1908, *Playthings Magazine* reported, "...prior to 1905, celluloid dolls were clumsy looking and could not withstand the knocking about that children gave them. Between 1905 and 1908, celluloid dolls improved in appearance and durability. Most of the Celluloid Dolls were made in Germany but many of them were painted by girls in Italy. All types of boys and girls were represented in celluloid dolls."

Production of celluloid was halted in the United States during the 1940s because of its tendency to burn or explode if placed near an open flame or high heat.

Because celluloid is easily broken and can become quite brittle, proper care helps a perfect celluloid example remain that way. Keep these dolls in a cool room with good ventilation. Celluloid is highly combustible, so never store a celluloid doll in a sealed case.

CELLULOID WEDDING COUPLE
2 3/4" **celluloid wedding couple,** original boxed pair, marked "Japan," painted eyes, in original outfits. .. **$75-$100/pair**

CELLULOID TWINS
3" **celluloid twins** with pacifiers, marked on back with a turtle, original pink and blue outfits. .... **$200-$250/pair**

CELLULOID GROUP
From left: **7 1/2" celluloid carnival Kewpie,** marked on back "GK" in a circle, painted features, side-glancing eyes, painted shoes, with original feathers and cane. ....**$50-$75**
8 1/2" German celluloid children, Hansel and Gretchen (#5934 and 5964), marked with a turtle in a diamond, jointed, marked "Made in Germany," in German outfits of felt, cotton, and leather, all original. ......**$150-$200 each**
8" celluloid rattle girl, dressed in red and white. ....**$20-$40**

CELLULOID PEASANT
9" celluloid doll, blue painted eyes, painted socks and shoes, wearing original traditional peasant outfit, tagged "Moll-6 origin TRACHTEN-Puppen." .... **$150-$200**

CELLULOID LADY
10" celluloid doll with jointed body, all original, tagged "Samaritaine Deluxe Paris." .... **$200-$225**

CELLULOID FOOTBALL PLAYER
13" celluloid head football player with Harvard "H," molded helmet, painted eyes, body stuffed with excelsior. .... **$250-$300**

CELLULOID PAIR
Left, 17" all celluloid jointed doll, marked with a turtle and "Schultz-Marae #43," molded hair, blue painted eyes, painted shoes and socks, redressed wearing a white eyelet baby dress. .... **$150-$200**
Right, **12" all celluloid baby,** marked with a stork (Parsons-Jackson, American, active 1910 to 1919), jointed body, blue painted eyes, open mouth with painted teeth, wearing a cream-colored embroidered net dress. .... **$250-$275**

CELLULOID BOY
19" celluloid head boy, marked "K(star)R 728-7 Germany 43/46," glass stationary eyes, open mouth with teeth, composition body, wearing a black velvet jacket, white straw hat and leather shoes. ....$750-$850

CELLULOID SWIVEL HEAD
27" painted celluloid swivel head, blue glass sleep eyes, open mouth with teeth and tongue, marked with a turtle and "47" on the neck, all composition jointed body, blonde wig with braids, wearing a white cotton dress and blue bonnet. .... **$400-$450**

HARD PLASTIC, LATEX, RUBBER, VINYL

When it was discovered that the milky white fluid produced by various seed plants—also known as latex—could be processed, it became the source of rubber and was later synthesized.

In 1837, Charles Goodyear received his first patent for a process that made rubber easier to work with. In 1843, Goodyear discovered that if sulfur was removed from rubber, then heated, it would retain its elasticity. This process, called vulcanization, made rubber waterproof and opened the door for an enormous market of rubber goods.

In the first half of the 20th century, plastics came into their own.

In 1909, inventor Leo Baekeland unveiled the world's first fully synthetic plastic—Bakelite—at a meeting of the New York chapter of the American Chemical Society. It could be fashioned into molded insulation, valve parts, pipe stems, billiard balls, knobs, buttons, knife handles, and all manner of items.

During the early 1920s, a rubber scientist named Waldo Semon stumbled onto a new material during his search for a synthetic adhesive. He experimented by making golf balls and shoe heels out of the material called polyvinyl chloride, or PVC.

But it wasn't until the late 1940s that plastics, rubber, and vinyl emerged as the basis for modern mass-produced dolls.

HARD PLASTIC, LATEX, RUBBER, VINYL DOLL MAKERS

Alexander Doll Co., founded 1923

A true American success story, the Alexander Doll Co. was established by the Alexander sisters—Beatrice Alexander Behman, Rose Alexander Schrecking, Florence Alexander Rapport, and Jean Alexander Disick. Their parents, Russian immigrants Maurice and Hannah Alexander, owned and operated the first doll hospital in the United States.

In 1929, a line of dolls appeared in trade catalogs advertised as "Madame Alexander." The following year the Alexander sisters expanded this line, now commonly known as "Madame Alexander Dolls."

Madame Alexander Dolls come in more than 7,000 different costumed personalities, so it's important to have the original costume and/or wrist tag to properly identify the dolls.

In 1995, the company was acquired by The Kalzen Breakthrough Partnership, a private capital fund. (Also see composition.)

MADAME ALEXANDER LITTLE GENIUS Two 7 1/2" **Madame Alexander "Little Genius" dolls,** hard plastic jointed bodies, blonde karakul wigs, bottle mouth, redressed, poor condition. ..... **$25-$50 each**

MADAME ALEXANDER GROOM
17" Madame Alexander hard plastic groom. In original clothing. Small scuff on left cheek. Fair condition. .... **$450-$500**

**MADAME
ALEXANDER
LITTLE WOMEN
14" Little Women doll,**
hard plastic, sleep eyes,
closed mouth, jointed
body, original red and
white striped cotton
dress. Fair condition.
.... **$300-$325**

MADAME ALEXANDER BRIDE AND GROOM
7 1/2" Madame Alexander bride and groom, hard plastic jointed bodies, all original, dress marked "Wendy Kin, Madame Alexander." Missing top hat. Fair to good condition. .... **$450-$500 each**

MADAME ALEXANDER GODEY LADY
20" Madame Alexander Godey Lady, blue sleep eyes, head marked
"Madame Alexander 1961," dress marked "Godey, Madame Alexander, NY,
USA." May be missing bag. .... **$500-$550**

MADAME ALEXANDER CISSY
20" Madame Alexander Cissy, hard plastic, all jointed including knees, sleep eyes, original hairdo, blue formal and fur. Missing necklace and evening bag. Appears somewhat faded. .... $400-$425

American Character Doll Co., 1919 to 1968

Located in New York, American Character Doll Co. started with composition dolls and later made a range of hard plastic and vinyl dolls. (Also see composition.)

AMERICAN CHARACTER BETSY MCCALL
8" Betsy McCall, jointed vinyl, sleep eyes, rooted hair, wearing original skating attire. Very good condition....... **$300-$350**

**AMERICAN CHARACTER
BETSY MCCALL**
13" Betsy McCall, head marked
1956, vinyl jointed body, wearing original blue cotton dress.
Appears to be original, fair
condition.................$250-$300

AMERICAN CHARACTER SWEET SUE

15" **American Character Sweet Sue,** hard plastic jointed body, blonde wig, redressed. Discolored, faded, "played with" condition.
.... **$100-$125**
If perfect ...... **$450-$500**

**AMERICAN CHARACTER
SWEET SUE**
20" **American Character
Sweet Sue,** hard plastic, sleep
eyes, jointed body, strawberry
blonde hair, redressed in cotton
print rickrack dress. Discolored,
faded, "played with" condition.
.................................$100-$125
If perfect .... $525-$550

AMERICAN CHARACTER TINY TEARS

13" American Character Tiny Tears, hard plastic head marked with patent number 20675644, bottle mouth and tear ducts, vinyl jointed body, all original. .... **$275-$350**

AMERICAN CHARACTER GIRL
14" American Character doll, all hard plastic, gray sleep eyes, original styled hair. Redressed, but nice display condition.......................... **$200-$225**

AMERICAN CHARACTER GIRL
18" American Character doll, all hard plastic, jointed body, sleep eyes, closed mouth, original taffeta plaid dress and hat. Appears original and in good condition with only slight fading... **$350-$400**

AMERICAN CHARACTER WHIMSIE
20" Whimsie character, marked "American Doll and Toy Corp., 1960 Series," dressed in black cap and gown with diploma. .... **$300-$325**

AMERICAN CHARACTER BRIDE
24" American Character bride, all hard plastic, jointed body, blue sleep eyes, original wedding dress and veil. Very good condition. .... **$500-$600**

AMERICAN CHARACTER TOODLES
24" **American Character Toodles,** vinyl head, hard plastic body with pin-jointed knees, sleep eyes, closed mouth, original cotton print dress. Apparently good condition. .... $350-$400

Arranbee Doll Co., 1922 to 1959

Founded in New York, Arranbee Doll Co. imported dolls, heads, and parts from Armand Marseille and Simon & Halbig. Arranbee later manufactured its own doll heads. Vogue Doll Co. acquired Arranbee in 1959 but continued to use the "R&B" mark until 1961. (Also see composition.)

Arranbee's most popular hard plastic dolls were Nanette and Nancy Lee, cousins to the composition Nancy Lee and Debu-Teen. Production of hard plastic dolls began in the 1940s. Although similar to composition in appearance, the thinner consistency of hard plastic allows a sharpness of detail that could not be achieved with composition.

During the 1950s, vinyl babies, toddlers, children, and teen-age style dolls were introduced.

An early synthetic material that looked and felt like human skin was sometimes called "Magic Skin." Over time, Magic Skin becomes unstable and deteriorates. (Also see composition.)

ARRANBEE JOINTED BODY 17 1/2" R&B hard plastic jointed body, sleep eyes, original gold shoes, green net dress, with green flowers on dress and in hair. Nice original condition. .... $450-$550

DeWees Cochran

DeWees Cochran began her doll career creating portrait dolls in New Hope, Pennsylvania. After World War II, she formed Dewees Cochran Dolls, Inc., and in 1947, the Cindy doll was introduced. In 1951-1952, Dewees developed the famous Grow-Up series of dolls: Susan Stormalong, Angela Appleseed, and Belinda Bunyan. In 1957, Peter Ponsett and Jefferson Jones joined the Grow-Up family. For the next five years, a new version of each doll was produced with features representing various stages of development. Grow-Up Dolls matured from childhood to adulthood in face and figure, growing from 12 1/2 to 18 inches.

SUSAN STORMALONG 11" **Susan Stormalong** by DeWees Cochran. With strawberry blonde hair and freckles, with the "SS" mark. Very good original condition. .... **$2,500-$3,000**

CINDY
14 1/2" Cindy by Dewees Cochran. Character girl with blonde human hair wig. Pristine original condition..$1,250-$1,500

ANGELA
15" Angela by Dewees Cochran. Character with blonde human hair, molded smiling open mouth with teeth, and painted blue eyes with lashes. Signed "58" on back of neck. Excellent and all original. ....**$2,800-$3,200**

PETER PONSETT
16" Peter Ponsett by Dewees Cochran. Dressed in gray wool jacket and shorts. Signed "PP55 #10." Excellent original condition. ....**$2,700-$3,000**

Eegee, founded 1917

Mr. and Mrs. E. Goldberger founded this company in Brooklyn, New York. The trademark EEGEE was adopted in 1923. Early dolls were marked "EG," followed by "E. Goldberger," and finally "Eegee" or occasionally "Goldberger."

**EEGEE
GROUCHO MARX**
32" Groucho Marx ven-
triloquist doll, marked
"Eegee Co.," vinyl head
and hands, cloth body.
.... $150-$175

Effanbee Doll Co., founded circa 1910

Effanbee is an acronym for Fleischaker & Baum, New York. The firm's Patsy doll was the first realistically proportioned American-made doll designed to resemble a real child. She was also the first doll for which companion dolls were created, and the first to have a wardrobe and fan club. In 1934, Effanbee introduced "Dydee," the first drink-and-wet doll. The company also imported and distributed cloth display or souvenir dolls made in Spain by Klumpe. (Also see cloth and composition.)

EFFANBEE HONEY
16" Honey doll, hard plastic jointed body, sleep eyes, original brown hair and clothing, including pink leather shoes and white socks. Beautiful doll in original condition; appears to have wrist tag.
.... **$500-$600**

Hasbro® Inc., founded 1923

Hasbro Inc. was originally known as Hassenfeld Bros., founded by Henry and Hillel Hassenfeld in Pawtucket, Rhode Island. The family-owned-and-operated toy business adopted the familiar Hasbro name following a division in the company. One branch went into the pencil box business, the other into the toy business.

In 1962, Hasbro's creative director, Don Levin, was approached by a television producer to develop a line of toys based on a pending television program about soldiers. The first G.I. Joe was introduced in 1964, and had 21 movable parts and realistic hair. He was named after the title character in the movie *The Story of G.I. Joe*. From the start, realism, simplicity, price, and a seemingly endless supply of accessories contributed to the success of the G.I. Joe figures. There were more than 500 G.I. Joe figures, vehicles, and auxiliary items introduced.

Production of G.I. Joe figures was suspended in 1978 due to an increase in the price of petroleum, a major component in the manufacturing of G.I. Joe. Hasbro currently offers new G.I. Joes in 3 3/4" and 12" sizes, along with dozens of related accessories. (For more information, visit Hasbro.com.)

HASBRO G.I. JOES

12" Hasbro G.I. Joes, including black adventurer with flocked hair, 1970, #7404, in tan Army fatigues; bandaged soldier with stretcher and medical equipment; and painted-hair Joe, 1964, in camouflage uniform. All three have scars on cheeks. Shown with footlocker made by Hassenfeld Bros., 1965.

Black figure .... **$150-$175**
Wounded soldier .... **$300-$350**
Camouflage soldier .... **$275-$325**

E.I. Horsman & Co., founded 1865

E.I. Horsman & Co., the well-known doll maker, was founded in New York by Edward Imeson Horsman. Beginning in the early 1900s, Horsman produced a variety of popular composition dolls.

Horsman is famous for marketing the Billiken doll, originally created by Florence Pretz of Kansas City, Missouri. It is reported that during the first six months of production, Horsman sold more than 200,000 Billikens. (Also see composition.)

HORSMAN CHILD
15" hard plastic child, circa 1952, marked "Horsman" on head, blue sleep eyes, open mouth with teeth, original wig, wearing a cotton print dress. Fair condition with good coloring and possibly original dress. .... **$200-$225**

HORSMAN
LUANN SIMMS
20 1/2" Horsman doll marked "LuAnn Simms," hard plastic, sleep eyes, open mouth with teeth, black hair, original red dress and white shoes. Original rare doll.
.... **$600-$750**

Ideal® Novelty and Toy Co., founded 1902

Morris Mitchom and A. Cohn founded the company initially to produce Mitchom's teddy bears.

Ideal began experimenting with hard plastic in 1936 and was the first to market a hard-plastic doll, resulting in Toni and the Play Pal Family. Play Pal children were designed according to measurements issued by the U.S. Bureau of Standards of Specifications. They could wear the clothing of a child at the age of three months, one year, two years, three years, and an older child of 10 or 11 years.

The first plastic doll was manufactured by Ideal in 1940, but was discontinued due to war restrictions on materials. Ideal's patent number for hard plastic was #2252077, and many different dolls can be found marked with this number. (Also see composition.)

IDEAL DOLL
14" Ideal doll, marked "P-90 Made in USA," all hard plastic, replaced wig, sleep eyes, redressed wearing an aqua satin and lace dress. .... **$100-$125**
If perfect .... **$600-$700**

IDEAL TONI
15" Ideal Toni doll, marked "P-91 Made in USA," all hard plastic, jointed body, sleep eyes, blonde hair, may be original red checked dress. Fair, "played with" condition. ....$250-$300

IDEAL HARRIET HUBBARD AYERS
16" Harriet Hubbard Ayers doll, head marked "Ideal, 16-P91," wearing original wedding dress and veil. This was a make-up doll. The faded appearance of face and lips is for the application of cosmetics. "As is" condition..**$75-$125**
If perfect, with boxed accessories of make-up ....**$600-$700**

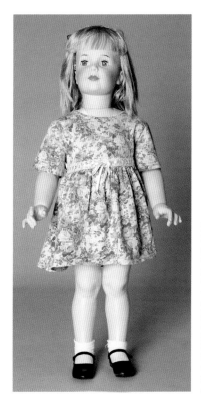

IDEAL
PATTY PLAY PAL
36" Patty Play Pal in original box. Beautiful, original, near mint vinyl doll in print dress with underwear, socks and shoes, blonde hair with red ribbon. Extremely bright facial coloring. Dress has slight soiling. Box is in good condition with tape marks and slight distressing.
.... **$1,500-$1,700**

**IDEAL
SHIRLEY TEMPLE
14" vinyl Shirley
Temple,** marked "1972
Ideal Toy ST-14 Corp.,
Hong Kong" and
"1972-5638," stationary
eyes, painted mouth,
rooted hair, wearing
original white dress
with red dots. Original,
good condition.
.... **$250-$300**

Kenner Parker Toys, Inc.

In 1985, Kenner became an independent company with two divisions, Parker Brothers and Kenner products. Kenner was once a subsidiary of General Mills. They produced many dolls as well as popular action figures.

KENNER BLYTHE
11 1/2" Blythe character doll, hard plastic head, vinyl body, marked "Blythe TM Kenner Prod., 1972, General Mills," pull string operates mechanism that changes color of eyes from brown to green to blue, in original red dress (poor condition). Although this doll is in poor condition, Blythe has recently achieved an almost cult-like following, ignited and fueled by the Internet. Consequently, even in this condition, Blythe has an inflated value.

.......................**$400-$500**
Blythe dolls in mint condition .....**$2,500-$2,800**
The demand for Blythe will most likely end soon, and the prices will drop quickly.

Mattel® Inc.,

Mattel Inc., founded by Harold Matson and Elliot Handler, derived its name from a combination of letters from the two partners' names. In 1945, Mattel established its headquarters in Hawthorne, California.

Mattel, the world's largest toy manufacturer, is probably best known for Barbie, along with her friends and family. Initially Mattel produced dollhouse furniture. They expanded to include music boxes, toy guns, and a host of dolls.

MATTEL CHATTY CATHY
20" Chatty Cathy, marked "Mattel," blue sleep eyes, dark rooted hair, wearing original red jacket, white dress and shoes. "Played with" condition. ....$100-$125
If perfect ....$400-$500

MATTEL CHARMIN' CHATTY
24" **Mattel talking "Charmin' Chatty"** with original box. Blonde doll
wearing red, white, and blue sailor's outfit. When pulling cord on back,
"Charmin' Chatty" talks (recording slightly unclear). Outfit has some
soiling. Good, original condition.. **$200-$300**

MATTEL ON PARADE
Barbie, Ken & Midge "On Parade" set with original box. In fine original
condition. Box shows wear to lid, and there is taping to corners.
.... **$4,000-$4,500/set**

BARBIE PONYTAIL #1
Barbie doll Ponytail #1, 1959. This doll appears to be in good to very good condition.
"Played with" condition .... $700-$900
Good to very good condition ....$3,000-$4,000
If perfect ....$9,000-$9,500

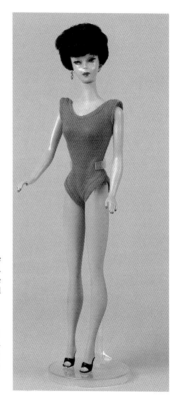

BUBBLECUT BARBIE
Mint-in-box, first-issue
Bubblecut Barbie doll.
This doll appears to be
in good to very good
condition.

"Played with" condition
.... **$200-$300**
Good to very good con-
dition............ **$500-$600**
If perfect ...... **$750-$900**

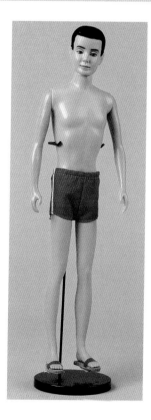

KEN
Ken doll was first issued in 1961. Note the flocked hair.
This doll appears to be in good to very good condition.

"Played with" condition ....
.... **$175-$250**
Good to very good condition
.... **$300-$350**
If perfect .... **$400-$500**

TWIST 'N TURN BARBIE
Twist 'n Turn Barbie doll
with pivoting waist, 1967.
This is an example of a
"played with" fair condition
doll with messed hair, shoes
and accessories missing.
"Played with" condition
.... **$200-$250**
If perfect .... **$600-$750**
With original trade-in box
.....................**$1,000-$1,200**

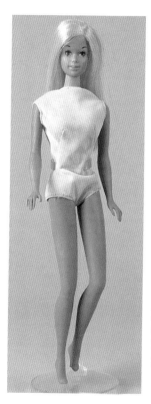

MALIBU BARBIE
The instantly popular Malibu Barbie doll, 1971. This is an example of a "played with" doll; shoes and accessories are missing and outfit shows wear.
"Played with" condition... **$40-$45**
If perfect .... **$75-$100**

The Pleasant Co., founded 1985

The Pleasant Co. was founded in 1985 by author-educator Pleasant T. Rowland in Middleton, Wisconsin. Rowland created the American Girl line of dolls, which also includes books and accessories. Mattel acquired the company in 1998.

PLEASANT CO. KRISTEN
Pleasant Co. American Girl "Kristen" with accessories. Variety of clothes, blue wooden trunk, dining room table, place settings, books, and accessories. Doll 18" tall. Like new, in boxes.
Doll as shown... **$400-$500**
With described extras .... **$900-$1,000**

Sasha Dolls, founded 1964

Designed by Swiss artist Sasha Morgenthaler (1893-1975), these dolls were mass-produced by Götz-Puppenfabrik, Rödental, Germany, beginning in 1964. Morgenthaler transferred the licensing rights to Trenton (sometimes spelled Trendon) Toy Ltd., Reddish, Stockport, England, which continued producing Sasha Dolls until the company went out of business in 1986.

The Gotz Dolls were marked "Sasha Series" within a circle on the back of the head. Also, the upper eyelids of the Gotz dolls are painted with a curved eyelid. Other Sasha Dolls are painted with a straighter eyelid line. All Sasha Dolls have a realistic body construction, allowing for a range of movement. Later Sasha dolls are unmarked except for a wrist tag.

A limited-edition series of dolls was produced between 1981 and 1986.

In 1995, Gotz again started making Sasha Dolls. The new Sashas, although similar in appearance to the earlier dolls, are marked with an incised circular logo between the shoulders, and the neck is incised "Gotz."

SASHA WHITE BABY
11" Sasha white baby. Blonde hair with knit white outfit, wrist tag, and original box. All original condition.....**250-$275**
Black baby ....**$300-$325**

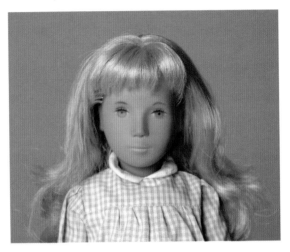

SASHA GIRL
16" Sasha girl. Long blonde hair, blue and white gingham romper, original wrist tag in original cylinder container. Overall fine condition. . **$400-$500**

SASHA BLACK CALEB
16" Trenton Sasha black Caleb. All original. Yellow spots on pants.
.... $450-$550

Terri Lee Co., 1946 to 1958

Violet Gradwohl established the Terri Lee Co. in Lincoln, Nebraska. The first dolls were made of composition and later hard plastic.

Gradwohl received a patent for a process used to create artificial hair wigs woven from Celanese yarn. She also designed the clothing with her daughter, Terri Lee, for whom the dolls were named.

A brother, Jerri Lee; sister, Baby Linda; and friends Bonnie Lu, Patty Jo, Benjie, and Nanooh (an Eskimo child) were introduced. All the dolls used the same basic doll mold—the only difference was wig types or facial painting. There are also a 10" Tiny Terri Lee and Tiny Jerri Lee, and a doll called Connie Lynn.

When the Terri Lee Co. factory in Lincoln was destroyed by fire, the firm relocated to Apple Valley, California.

Several copies of Terri Lee dolls have been produced. Many were made during the early 1950s at the peak of Terri Lee's popularity.

TERRI LEE BRIDE
16" Terri Lee bride (1951), blonde hair, original dress and veil. Original fair to good condition. $450-$550
.... **$450-$550**

JERRI LEE

16" Jerri Lee, hard plastic, jointed body, brown painted eyes, fur hair, wearing original fireman's hat and saddle shoes, redressed. "Played with" condition. .. **$350-$400**
If perfect .... **$900-$1,000**

Vogue Dolls, Inc., founded circa 1918

Jennie H. Graves started the company in Somerville, Massachusetts, focusing on the production of doll clothing until the mid-1930s. Graves initially bought undressed bisque dolls from German manufacturers, dressing them in her designs, and reselling them.

In 1948, the Ginny-type doll was introduced as a composition doll, known as "Toddles."

Several Vogue Dolls were originally Arranbee Dolls. Vogue purchased Arranbee in 1957, but the dolls continued to be marked and sold as Arranbee until as late as 1961.

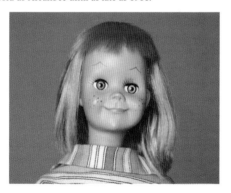

VOGUE BRICKETTE
22" vinyl "Brickette" doll, 1961 by the Vogue Doll Co., character girl has green flirty/sleep eyes, bright orange hair, and freckles. Comes with fashion sunglasses. Appears in very good original condition. .... **$250-$300**

Wooden Dolls

Figures carved from wood are some of the oldest and most sought-after of all dolls. From fragile 17th century examples to contemporary artist creations, such dolls represent a special collecting challenge.

Prone to damage because of the expansion and contraction of the wood, painted surfaces are often crazed and crackled.

While many vintage dolls employed some wood in their construction, this section focuses on dolls with carved and shaped wooden heads, and bodies constructed with significant wooden components.

WOODEN WILLIAM & MARY DOLL

17" English wood William & Mary doll. From the late 17th century and appears to be in all original, untouched condition. Finely molded facial details including elaborately carved ears and painted eyes, mouth, and cheeks. Fingers are well defined and carved (damage to three fingers on right hand). Wooden legs are covered in green silk with leather shoes. Chartreuse silk dress covers a multi-colored linen skirt with an aqua blue blouse, gauze apron, and a bonnet. Original skull cap intact but majority of hair is missing. Two scuffs to doll's left cheek. Wonderful, rare collectible. Dolls of this caliber: .... **$50,000-$70,000**

WOODEN QUEEN ANNE-TYPE
19" Queen Anne-type wooden doll. With brown pupil-less faceted glass eyes, carved facial details, molded breastplate, wooden arms, and jointed wooden legs. Undergarment is a cotton print that is covered by a quilted chartreuse leaded satin skirt that is, in turn, covered by an aqua leaded satin dress and topped with a gauze coverlet enhanced with embroidery. Brown human hair wig (replaced) and lace bonnet with silk pink and silver brocade ribbon. Small amount of touch-up to face. .... **$20,000-$22,000**

WOODEN TOUT EN BOIS
Pair of "tout en bois" (all wood) babies. Both have brown glass eyes, one with painted hair, and one with mohair. Doll with mohair wig has a split at the right eye. Both have some flaking to bodies.

With wig .... $550-$600
Painted hair, "as is" condition .... $400-$425

SHADOW BOX OF WOODEN DOLLS
Shadow box display of early wooden dolls. According to paper on rear of shadow box, these carved wooden "Peg Dolls" are probably of German manufacture, circa 1840s. Thirteen "woodens," approximately 1" to 4" tall. Case size approximately 8 1/2" by 12" by 3". It appears that there has been paint restoration to many of the dolls. This type of collection always appeals to collectors. .... **$750-$1,000/set**

Door of Hope Dolls, 1901 to 1949

These dolls were made in Shanghai and Canton, China, at a Protestant mission called the Door of Hope, established to rescue and educate destitute children and slave girls.

At the Door of Hope Mission, the girls were taught needlework, embroidery, knitting, and other skills used to make doll clothing. A girl working five days a week could complete one doll a month. The head, hands, and arms to the elbow were carved of pear wood. The smooth wood was not painted or varnished. The hair, eyes, and lips were painted. A few of the dolls had fancy buns or flowers carved into their heads. Most have hands with rounded palms and separate thumbs, although some have been found with cloth stub hands. Cloth bodies were stuffed with raw cotton donated to the mission by local textile factories. The elaborate handmade costumes are exact copies of clothing worn by the Chinese people. Dolls were unmarked or labeled "Made in China."

DOOR OF HOPE GRANDMOTHER
11" Door of Hope Chinese grandmother. Intricately carved wood, with facial detail, with silk outfit and headpiece (open at back but covering ears and exposing the back of head, which depicts a bun and thinning hair), and carved wooden arms. Significant fading to front of jacket.
.... $2,300-$2,500

DOOR OF HOPE BRIDEGROOM
11 1/2" Door of Hope bridegroom. Intricately carved wood with elaborate plum silk outfit and hat with carved wooden arms. Fine original condition.
.... **$2,000-$2,400**

DOOR OF HOPE MOURNER
11 1/2" Door of Hope Chinese male mourner. Intricately carved wood with fancy muslin and burlap clothing, including hat, and carved wooden arms. Fine original condition. ....$2,500-$2,700

A. Schoenhut & Co., founded 1872

Located in Philadelphia, Albert Schoenhut came from a family of German toy makers. He came to the United States at the age of 17, and at 22 established his own toy factory. Schoenhut's first toy was a piano.

The Humpty Dumpty Circus, introduced in 1903, probably included Schoenhut's first attempt at doll making. At about this time, Schoenhut introduced the Chinaman, Hobo, Negro Dude, Farmer, Milkmaid, and Max and Mortiz. Rolly-Dollys were patented in 1908.

In 1909, Schoenhut filed a patent application for his swivel, spring-jointed dolls, but the patent was not granted until 1911.

After Albert Schoenhut's death in 1912, his six sons took over: Harry, Gustav, Theodore, Albert Jr., William, and Otto. The new directors introduced an infant doll with curved limbs in 1913. The dolly faced all-wooden dolls produced in 1915 had rounded eyes, advertised as "imitation glass" (as opposed to intaglio eyes), and mohair wigs. A series of 19" tall older boy dolls, called "Manikins," commonly dressed as athletes, was also introduced in 1915.

Walking dolls, jointed at the shoulder and hip only, were introduced in 1919. Cloth-bodied mama dolls and a less expensive line of dolls with elastic joints were marketed in 1924.

SCHOENHUT DOLLY FACE
15" Schoenhut dolly face. Carved wood with molded and painted teeth, blonde mohair wig (replaced) on a jointed wood body. Painted eyes and finely feathered eyebrows and has been redressed. Some paint crazing to cheeks. .... **$700-$900**

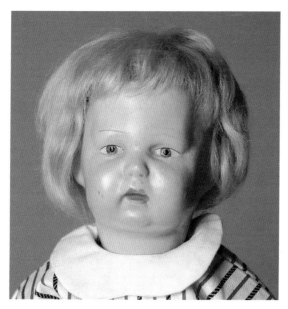

SCHOENHUT MAMA
16" Schoenhut "mama" doll. Blonde mohair wig and blue painted eyes on a cloth body with wood hands and "mama" cry box, wearing new striped romper. Light crazing, original paint, skullcap is original, but mohair has been attached. Crier is in working condition. .... **$500-$700**

Other Dolls

Peddler Dolls

During the late 18th and early 19th centuries, peddler dolls were popular fashion accessories. Frequently created to exhibit a woman's artistic talents, a peddler doll depicted a traveling vendor and served as a decorating accent, sometimes placed under a glass dome in a prominent location.

Itinerant traders traveled over Europe and the United States, but it was the English peddler doll for which there seemed a special fascination. Women traveled about the countryside selling needles, pins, and other small articles. These women were called "Notion Nannies," and were familiar figures in English country districts.

The weathered and wrinkled dolls made to resemble these travelers were made of cloth, leather, wood, papier-mâché, wax, cork, china, dried apples, and even breadcrumbs. The bodies were usually wooden or cloth-covered wire. The Notion Nannies—with traditional red cape, calico dress gathered to expose a black quilted slip, white apron, and black silk bonnet over a white-laced "mob" cap—were a particular favorite.

Although the majority of vintage peddler dolls were homemade, C. H. White of Portsmouth, England, advertised commercially made dolls. The marbleized paper-cover base and "C. H. White/Milton/Portsmouth" label allows for easy identification.

PEDDLER DOLL
10" wax peddler doll with wares. A wonderfully presented peddler in good condition with an incredible assortment of miniatures. Most pieces appear to be original. Large split at forehead continuing down through eye. The damage has little effect on this wonderful example of an early peddler doll.
....$4,000-$5,000

Glossary of Doll Terms

Applied Ears: Ears that are molded separately and affixed to the head.

Appropriately Dressed: Clothing that fits the time period and doll style.

Ball-Jointed Body: Doll body of wood and composition, jointed at shoulder, elbows, wrists, hip, and knees, allowing movement.

Bébé: French dolly-faced doll.

Bébé Tout en Bois: Doll all of wood.

Bent-Limb Baby Body: Five-piece baby body of composition with curved arms and legs, jointed at shoulder and hip.

Bisque: Unglazed porcelain.

Blown Glass Eyes: Hollow eyes of blue, brown, or gray.

Breather Dolls: Dolls with pierced or open nostrils.

Brevete: French marking indicating a registered patent.

Bte: Patent registered.

Caracul: Lamb's skin used to make wigs. (Also spelled karakul.)

Character Doll: Dolls molded to look lifelike; may be infants, children, or adults.

Child Doll: Typical dolly-face dolls.

China: Glazed porcelain.

Composition: A wood-based material.

Crazing: Fine lines that develop on the painted surface of composition.

D.E.P.: A claim to registration.

Dolly Face: Typical child doll face.

D.R.G.M.: German marking indicating a registered design.

Feathered Brows: Eyebrows painted with many tiny strokes.

Five-Piece Body: Body composed of torso, arms, and legs.

Fixed Eyes: Eyes set in a stationary position.

Flange Neck: Doll's neck with ridge and holes at the base for sewing onto a cloth body.

Flirty Eyes: Eyes that move from side to side when head is moved.

Flocked Hair: A coating of short fibers glued to a doll's head to represent hair.

Ges (Gesch): German marking indicating a registered design.

Googly Eyes: Large, round eyes looking to the side.

Gutta-percha: A pinkish-white rubbery, hard, fibrous substance once used to make dolls, bodies, and parts.

Hard Plastic: Material used after 1948. It is very hard with excellent impressions and good color.

Hina-Ningyo: Japanese festival doll.

Huminals: Figures having both human and animal characteristics.

Ichimatus: Japanese play doll.

Intaglio Eyes: Sunken, rather than cut, eyes that are then painted.

Kabuto: Japanese warrior or helmet for a Japanese warrior.

Kid Body: Doll body made of leather.

Lady Doll: Doll with adult face and body proportions.

Magic Skin: A rubbery material used for dolls. They age poorly, becoming dark and deteriorating as the surface turns soft and sticky.

Mask Face: A stiff face that covers only the front of a doll's head.

Mohair Wig: Wig made from very fine goat's hair.

Mold Number: Impressed or embossed number that indicates a particular design.

Open Mouth: Lips parted with opening cut into the bisque. Teeth usually show.

Open/Closed Mouth: Molded mouth appears open, but no opening is cut into the bisque.

Painted Bisque: Paint that is not baked into body; brighter in color, but can be rubbed off.

Painted Eyes: Flat or rounded painted eyes.

Paperweight Eyes: Blown glass eyes with an added crystal to the top, resulting in a look with depth and great realism.

Papier-mâché: Material made of paper pulp and glue.

Pate: Covering for the opening in a doll head. May be made of cardboard, cork, or plaster.

Peppering: Tiny black specks in the slip of many older bisque or china dolls.

Personality Doll: Doll molded and fashioned to resemble a famous person.

Pierced Ears: Holes in a doll's ear lobes. Hole goes all the way through the lobe.

Pierced-in Ears: Hole for earring passing through doll's earlobe and straight into doll's head.

Pouty: Closed-mouth doll with a solemn or petulant expression.

Pug or Pugged Nose: Small, button, slightly turned-up nose.

Queue: Asian hairstyle of a single plait.

Regional Costume: A traditional costume worn in a specific region or country.

Reproduction: A doll produced from a mold taken from an existing doll.

Rub: A spot where the color has worn away.

Sakura-Ningyo: Traditional Japanese cherry doll.

S.G.D.G.: Registered but without government guarantee.

Shoulder Head: Head and shoulder in one piece.

Shoulder Plate: Shoulder portion with socket for head.

Socket Head: Head with neck that fits into a shoulder plate or the opening of a body.

Solid-dome: Head with no crown opening. May have painted hair or wear a wig.

Stationary Eyes: Glass eyes that do not sleep; also known as staring eyes.

Stockinette: Soft jersey fabric used for dolls.

Toddler Body: A short, chubby body of a toddler; often with diagonal joints at hips.

Turned Head: Shoulder head with head slightly turned.

Vinyl: Material used after 1950.

Walker Body: Head moves from side to side when legs are made to walk.

Watermelon Mouth: A closed, smiling mouth, usually with a single line.

Weighted Eyes: Sleep eyes that operated by means of a weight attached to a wire frame holding the eyes.

Index

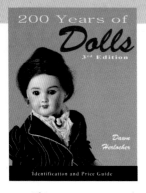

200 Years of
Dolls
3rd Edition

Dawn Herlocher

Identification and Price Guide

Reap the Rewards of Savvy Doll Decisions

200 Years of Dolls
Identification and Price Guide
3rd Edition
by Dawn Herlocher

This easy-to-use comprehensive identification and value guide helps you enjoy doll collecting more, with tips for avoiding bad investments, and extensive pricing and identification information. From novice collector to appraiser, wherever your doll collecting takes you, this full-color book is your connection to expert advice and information.

In this new edition you'll discover:

- More than 5,000 detailed doll listings covering everything from cloth to molded dolls, and more
- Updated pricing displayed in easy-to-follow value grids
- 400+ brilliant full-color photos and new manufacturer marks listings to aid in identification

Celebrate doll collecting with this invaluable guide!

Softcover • 8¼ x 10⅞ • 416 pages • 400 color photos • Item# DOLY3 • $29.99